Culturally Responsive Teaching and Reflection in Higher Education

Culturally Responsive Teaching and Reflection in Higher Education explores how postsecondary educators can develop their own cultural awareness and provide inclusive learning environments for all students. Discussing best practices from the Cultural Literacy Curriculum Institute at Lesley University, faculty and administrators who are committed to culturally responsive teaching reflect on how to create an inclusive environment and how educators can cultivate the skills, attitudes, and knowledge necessary for implementing culturally responsive curriculum and pedagogy. Rather than a list of "right answers," essays in this important resource integrate discussion and individual reflection to support educators to enhance skills for responding effectively to racial, cultural, and social difference in their personal and professional contexts. This book is an excellent starting point or further enrichment resource to accompany program or institutional diversity and inclusion efforts.

Sharlene Voogd Cochrane is Professor Emeritus of Interdisciplinary Studies at Lesley University, USA.

Meenakshi Chhabra is Associate Professor of Interdisciplinary Studies at Lesley University, USA.

Marjorie A. Jones is Professor of Education and Writing at Lesley University, USA.

Deborah Spragg is Director of Field Training and Assistant Professor of Expressive Therapies at Lesley University, USA.

Culturally Responsive Teaching and Reflection in Higher Education

Promising Practices From the Cultural Literacy Curriculum Institute

Edited by
Sharlene Voogd Cochrane,
Meenakshi Chhabra,
Marjorie A. Jones,
and Deborah Spragg

Routledge
Taylor & Francis Group

NEW YORK AND LONDON

First published 2017
by Routledge
711 Third Avenue, New York, NY 10017

and by Routledge
2 Park Square, Milton Park, Abingdon, Oxon, OX14 4RN

*Routledge is an imprint of the Taylor & Francis Group, an
informa business*

© 2017 Taylor & Francis

Library of Congress Cataloging-in-Publication Data
Names: Cochrane, Sharlene Voogd.
Title: Culturally responsive teaching and reflection in higher
    education: promising practices from the Cultural Literacy
    Curriculum Institute / by Sharlene Voogd Cochrane, Meenakshi
    Chhabra, Marjorie A. Jones, and Deborah Spragg.
Description: New York: Routledge, 2017. | Includes bibliographical
    references.
Identifiers: LCCN 2016050429 | ISBN 9781138240544 (hardback) |
    ISBN 9781315283333 (ebook) | ISBN 9781315283319 (epub) |
    ISBN 9781315283302 (mobipocket)
Subjects: LCSH: College teaching. | Multicultural education. |
    Culturally relevant pedagogy.
Classification: LCC LB2331 .C52357 2017 | DDC 378.1/25—dc23
LC record available at https://lccn.loc.gov/2016050429

ISBN: 978-1-138-24054-4 (hbk)
ISBN: 978-1-315-28333-3 (ebk)

Typeset in Times New Roman
by Apex CoVantage, LLC

Contents

Preface: An Invitation for Dialogue

The world in which you were born is just one model of reality.
Other cultures are not failed attempts at being you:
they are unique manifestations of the human spirit.
　　　　　　　　　　　—Wade Davis, anthropologist and ethnobiologist

We invite readers to join us, through these essays, to explore and critically examine faculty experiences in culturally responsive teaching and creating equitable, inclusive teaching and learning experiences. In doing so, we prepare to better serve students in our diverse, complex communities and world. We offer the essays as encouragement for a wide variety of college and university faculty to be reflective, aware, and intentional in their teaching about race, class, religion, disability, and other social and cultural identities. A community of colleagues gathering together to engage with these topics is key for meeting the challenges we face as educators today, especially as we build diverse, equitable teaching/learning environments.

The contributors for this book participated in the Culture Literacy Curriculum Institute (CLCI), a faculty professional development program at Lesley University created to expand and sustain culturally responsive and inclusive teaching and learning practices and environment throughout the University. The structure provided time, space, and resources for a community of colleagues from varied disciplines and programs to gather. Within this time and space, faculty considered the implications, challenges, and opportunities for increasing their culturally responsive teaching.

Two years ago, a group of faculty from CLCI designed a semester study group to continue our discussions. We began to write about our experiences and about the resulting changes in our own attitudes, curriculum, and pedagogy. This writing coalesced into the CLCI Writing Project, with regular meetings of interested faculty and discussions that shaped our essays, reflecting our rich, multifaceted dialogue. We wrote as a way to explore how personal narratives of diverse faculty at a predominantly white institution can inform culturally responsive practice.

The Writing Project captured our personal and professional experiences linked to Institute readings, exercises, and learning. Through this narrative process, we imagined a book that invites faculty in other colleges and universities to use our explorations and questions in their own efforts to reflect and learn more deeply about themselves and their teaching practice.

Like many educators, including those eager to address racial and social equity, we have often felt a lack of language, knowledge, and confidence to effectively bring these discussions and interactions to our students. Understanding our own backgrounds, assumptions, and racial and cultural awareness has been a significant component of building our skills and abilities. The CLCI supported our growth in these areas.

The Writing Project contributors come from every school in the University and are a diverse range of ethnicities, races, ages, academic specialties, and perspectives. One identity we share: we are all women. While men as well as women participated in the CLCI, Lesley has many programs in education, arts, and human services and, as such, has historically had more female faculty than male. The invitation to participate in the Writing Project was university-wide; more women than men responded.

Lesley University, like the majority of colleges and universities in the United States, has predominantly white students, faculty, and staff. Committed to expanding the diversity of the academic community, it has established efforts in terms of faculty and student recruitment, retention, culture audits, and diversity programs and conversations. Still, the culture is shaped by its white, privileged identity, and continues to face the challenges of making its stated goals a reality. The Introduction discusses this in more detail.

This collection of essays invites readers to take responsibility for their role and contribution to creating culturally responsive learning environments. We provide accessible narratives, reflective materials, and teaching applications appropriate for individual teachers or for study groups and professional development activities. The book can serve as an excellent starting point or further enrichment resource to accompany program or institutional diversity and inclusion efforts. Rather than a list of "to do's" or "right answers," the essays integrate discussion, individual reflection, and questions we still have.

The essays are organized into three sections: Knowing Ourselves, Pedagogy and Power, and Practice in Community.

In the first section, "Knowing Ourselves," authors focus on how they have come to more fully understand themselves in terms of race or class. Sharlene Voogd Cochrane describes several "Steppingstones" toward her sense of white identity, and the implications for her current teaching about race and social justice. Julie A. Stanwood looks at her growing sense of her own white privilege, and how white teachers can interact around social identities with undergraduate white students who may not have had many experiences reflecting, especially about race and religion. Michaela Kirby demonstrates how teaching about class changed as she acknowledged and reflected on her own class background and experiences.

The second section, "Pedagogy and the *Other*," presents experiences around power and the "other." Meenakshi Chhabra, through her role as the *other* in shifting cultural contexts, grapples with issues of race and religion. As a university faculty in the United States conducting research in her home country, India, she uncovers the dynamic processes of being stigmatized and stigmatizing and the challenge of seeing oneself as having a capacity for both, which she articulates as "human fragility."

Coleen O'Connell introduces ways in which faculty and students can change their relationships with Indigenous peoples with examples from her teaching from an ecological framework. The final essay begins with personal strategies M. Francine Jennings has developed for addressing white students' curiosities about her status as an African American faculty. She further explains how she uses these curiosities to assist students in becoming more culturally proficient when working with children in the classroom.

The third section, "Practice in Community," presents narratives focused on particular disciplines or cultural groups within the University. Marjorie A. Jones invites college faculty to consider ways in which faculty promote self-reflection about race and culture for themselves and their students, informing their professional practices, from the perspective of student teachers in the U.S. and human service professionals in Guyana. Deborah D. Wright uses the poem "Where I'm From" as a rich resource for adult learners and analyzes its power for these returning students. She reflects on teaching decisions she has made as a result.

Deborah Spragg reflects on ways in which cultural assumptions may be explored through a discipline-specific lens. Graduate students in the expressive therapies must consider their choice of art materials when working with any client; both the therapeutic work grounded in the arts and the art materials themselves are rooted in a cultural context. Janet Sauer examines her personal journey toward a belief that advocacy for the inclusion of students with disabilities in community and educational contexts is a social justice issue and is necessary for a healthy democracy. She models inclusive practice in higher education, paying particular attention to the intersections among race, class, culture, and dis/ability as social constructs.

The essays are examples of promising practices and valuable questions for faculty in implementing and deepening their commitment to cultural literacy and culturally responsive teaching. We hope you'll join the conversation.

Reference

Davis, Wade. (n.d.). Quotes. Retrieved from https://www.goodreads.com/author/quotes/4652058

Acknowledgments

Our CLCI Writing Group is deeply grateful to many supporters who have made this book possible, especially: B.J. Addison Reid, Director for Equal Opportunity and Inclusion at Lesley University, a staunch and tireless advocate and co-facilitator for the Cultural Literacy Curriculum Institute; Kathy Holmes, research librarian extraordinaire, for providing resources and being a lively participant in our Writing Group conversations, ideas, and learning; the many faculty members who participated in the CLCI and their ongoing commitment to culturally responsive teaching; and the Office of the Provost and each of the School Deans who provided the Institutional support necessary for a project of this scope.

Thank you!

1 Introduction

Cultural Literacy, Cultural Humility, and Reflection

Sharlene Voogd Cochrane,
Meenakshi Chhabra, Marjorie A. Jones,
and Deborah Spragg

The United States will soon become a majority-minority nation. Analysis of the 2010 Census indicates a shift in the nation's racial makeup that is reshaping schools, work places, and the electorate. Where now the white population of the United States is 61.5 percent and people of color are 38.5%, within the next generation, the white population will be under 50 percent. The Brookings Institute reports that currently more than 45 percent of students in K–12 are students of color. In the next five years nonwhite children will surpass 50 percent, and by 2039, racial and ethnic minorities will make up a majority of the U.S. working-age population (2013).

These statistics have significant implications for educational practice in colleges and universities; it is increasingly important that faculty, students, and staff respond effectively across racial, religious, and social difference. Colleges and universities face increasingly complex issues that are the focus of current campus concern, including protests demanding better relationships between white students and faculty and students of color, a resurgence of student organizing in response to recent current events and the Black Lives Matter movement, and recognizing the reality and seriousness of continuing racial discrimination in the United States.

These challenges are particularly relevant for primarily white institutions (PWIs): the majority of colleges and universities in the country. In fact, responding to increasing diversity has been on the agenda of many colleges and universities, and the efforts to create inclusive environments produce a lively current discourse. Our institution has been committed to increasing the cultural and economic diversity of the student body, with a goal of having students and faculty of color comprise 20 percent of the total student and faculty population. The numbers have been slowly growing, with the annual "Diversity Score Card" showing employees of color in 2010 at 14.5 percent, and at 18.5 percent in 2014. Students of color increased from 9.3 percent in 2010 to 15.8 percent in 2014 (Addison-Reid, 2014).

Still, Lesley, like most other colleges and universities, remains a primarily white institution. Gusa posits that there is a "White Institutional Presence," or an ideology within the traditions, practices, and perceptions about knowledge that is taken for granted at such institutions as the norm. Primarily white institutions must not only serve more students of color, but they must serve them well. They also must understand and challenge the effect of whiteness on the curriculum, pedagogy, and student experiences (Gusa, 2010).

Faculty members face the challenge of knowing more about the experience of students of color in PWIs and supporting the culturally responsive skills and attitudes of white students. This is true for faculty in all subjects, disciplines, and coursework, in order to implement cultural literacy and culturally responsive teaching fully into the institutional environment. Our book makes a unique contribution to this emerging discourse by presenting the narratives of faculty actively engaged in the opportunities and challenges of culturally responsive teaching.

Cultural Literacy, Cultural Humility

The Culture Literacy Curriculum Institute (CLCI) content and format and our written narratives are based on the understanding that three foci are critical for increasing culturally responsive teaching in primarily white colleges and universities:

1. individual awareness and growth;
2. implications for curriculum and pedagogy, including issues of power and structural racism; and
3. institutional cultural climate.

We have found the concepts of literacy and humility applied to social and cultural realities an effective way to deepen these conversations.

"Literacy" usually refers to the development of reading, writing, and language skills, while "cultural literacy" captures our goal of building skills in understanding and communicating across varieties of cultural difference and experience. Cultural literacy is a critical set of attitudes, knowledge, skills, and commitments in negotiating the network of beliefs, values, and characteristics that determine a group's identity and relationships.

CLCI participants read several books in common. Our initial Institute texts included *Educating Culturally Responsive Teachers: A Coherent Approach.* Villegas and Lucas describe culturally responsive teachers as having a sociocultural consciousness, affirming views of students from diverse backgrounds, and embracing constructivist views of teaching and learning. Such educators are familiar with their students' prior knowledge and beliefs and design instruction that builds on what students know, yet goes beyond the familiar. These educators sense a responsibility for bringing about educational change so that schools are more responsive to diverse student needs (2002, p. xiv).

We also read *Transforming Classroom Culture: Inclusive Pedagogical Practices* (2011), in which editors Dallalfar, Kingston-Mann, and Sieber gather writing from faculty primarily from Lesley University and UMass Boston. Aligning with the culturally responsive concepts, the authors highlight their experiences of bringing inclusive theories to teaching practices within their specific disciplines.

"Cultural humility" has deepened our understanding of the ways such work can be effective. A video by Vivian Chavez and Melanie Tervalon introduces participants to the three components of the concept, which align well with the design of the CLCI. The focus on cultural learning as lifelong and related to power issues, plus the importance of institutional support for culturally responsive teaching, spoke to our experiences.

The first component of cultural humility is the commitment to lifelong learning and critical self-reflection, especially around social identities. Cultural humility requires that each of us respond to culture as an ongoing process, accompanied by regular self-reflection. How carefully am I listening? What more can I learn?

One of our Writing Group participants tells this story as an example of her realizing the need for ongoing cultural learning:

> We sat crowded around the dining room table in the dimly lit center of the pueblo home, large earthen-ware pots on the kitchen counters and clay sculpture adorning the corner tables and shelves near-by. While hot and dry outside, with a dusty wind blowing, inside cool, fresh air surrounded us as we listened intently to the older woman sharing her home with us. Our class of graduate and undergraduate students traveled from Boston to study the "Cultures and Traditions of the Southwest," and one of the highlights was a visit to Santa Clara Pueblo and our host and guide, who shared her insights about family, women's roles, and the experiences of her community, including the pottery-making for which her family excelled.
>
> As she responded to questions, she mentioned a previous visit, looked at me and hesitated. Thinking she had forgotten my name, I reminded her as she continued her conversation. Later in the discussion, this happened again, and again I reminded her of my name. The visit ended with a group photograph; then the students walked ahead toward the van. As I walked by the pots of plants on the small patio and said my goodbyes, she quietly said, "My friend, I know your name. We just talk more slowly in our culture." Her words, though gentle, carried a forceful message. Shocked and chagrined, I realized that I jumped in with my

Western, fast-speaking assumptions, and had not respected her pace, her story. I thanked her for her comment and slowly walked back to the van, embarrassed and troubled. I was still learning to listen to those whose practices were different, and appreciate those differences.

A second quality of cultural humility is the need to recognize and disrupt power imbalances. Such imbalances exist between individuals according to social identities and roles, and between individuals, groups, and institutions. It is vital to positive relationships that such power imbalances be acknowledged and challenged. Power is often an unspoken element in learning environments; faculty in colleges and universities make a number of choices when they teach that reflect their own power, as well as their practice of cultural humility.

While we look to create the quality of cultural humility within our students and ourselves, we also need to fully assess how we express power relationships within our teaching. Working with English language learners (ELL) affords one example of recognizing the power imbalances between teachers and students, and the privileging of English speakers:

> One faculty recalled a bright, energetic, fun-loving student in her class, committed to her education, comfortable, expressive, and a conceptual thinker in her home language of Spanish. In English she struggled to express the depth and thoughtfulness of her ideas. Her writing contained English grammar errors and awkward sentence structure. A constant tension existed between her critical thinking ability and academic writing. The faculty member could have said she was not capable of the coursework, and given her a low grade. As a culturally humble educator, she also had the power to give extensive feedback and time to rewrite and rewrite, allowing her student to continue working on her English writing challenges. In making this choice the student could own and express her academic power, inviting her into a process that both acknowledged her strengths and her need to improve her communication skills.

The third requirement for cultural humility is institutional accountability. Responding to cultural difference is a charge to individuals; at the same time, we are part of larger institutions, and many times institutional structures, environments, values, and experiences shape our responses and actions. Accountability includes supporting ways for faculty to talk and develop together and engaging administrators who can make the budget and resource decisions to prioritize this work.

The environments we work and learn within, especially in groups such as faculty organizations, program developers, and university administrators, must set a standard of openness, willingness to learn, reflective engagement, and acknowledgment of power realities. The CLCI has been an example of institutional support and collaboration, from the Provost's Office and the Office of Equal Opportunity and Inclusion, the Lesley University Diversity Council, faculty and Deans in each school, and collegial leadership assumed by individual faculty.

Developing Cultural Humility: Embracing Race, Privilege and Power, edited by Miguel Gallardo, has added to our understanding of this process and underscores the lifelong weaving of teaching and learning that cultural humility requires. First, we develop the cultural humility capacity in ourselves, our willingness to learn, self-reflect, and acknowledge power dynamics. Then we bring this practice and awareness to our classes, both in course content and pedagogy. We model and address these attitudes and skills with transparency, encourage all voices, and respect individual stories.

One of the critiques our Writing Group raised about cultural humility is that "humility" often suggests passivity, accepting, and not speaking up. It seemed more useful as a goal for white faculty in approaching difference, rather than for the faculty of color. We agreed the notion of "cultural courage" seemed equally necessary for speaking and acting in difficult situations.

As our discussion evolved about both humility and courage, we were struck by the way Parker Palmer, in *Healing the Heart of Democracy*, writes about humility and chutzpah:

> By *chutzpah* I mean knowing that I have a voice that needs to be heard and the right to speak it. By *humility* I mean accepting the fact that my truth is always partial and may not be true at all—so I need to listen with openness and respect, especially to "the other," as much as I need to speak my own voice with clarity.
>
> (2011, p. 43)

A similar dynamic is captured in the term "critical humility," which describes the paradox necessary for white people to engage in anti-racism:

> We define critical humility as the practice of remaining open to the fact that our knowledge is partial and evolving while at the same time being committed to speaking up and taking action in the world based on our current knowledge, however imperfect . . . In other words, we strive toward being a "good white person" while trying not to fall into the trap of thinking we actually have become that person.
>
> (European-American Collaborative Challenging Whiteness, 2012, p. 2)

Reflection and Relationships

Faculty of color (FOC) at primarily white institutions bring real-life experience to other faculty and both white students and students of color who may not have had close interactions with FOC in higher education. FOC therefore make a critical and significant contribution to the environment and dialogue on culture and diversity. There are challenges embedded in this experience, but practices such as developing syllabi jointly and co-teaching teams of white faculty and FOC are strategies that deepen faculty relationships. Opportunities such as the CLCI also support such relationships.

As colleagues in the Writing Project, both white and faculty of color, we held many conversations about culture and difference. We laughed, cried, and expressed anger about injustices and narrow-minded or prejudiced comments and situations in our lives and in our classrooms. We began to feel comfortable enough with each other to confront our blindness and hubris, and to talk honestly about our mistakes, insights, and moments of success. We experienced the importance of deeper faculty relationships as a significant component in developing an attitude of cultural literacy, cultural humility, and courage. These relationships encouraged honesty and actively challenged us to grow.

The significance of relationship raises a question about how cultural humility develops. In our society, much that passes for news and entertainment contains stereotypes, misinformation, and outright racist, negative images. Unless a white person has opportunities to interact with those of other races, languages, and cultural groups, he or she can remain recruited into racism and closed-mindedness. It takes intention and courage to go beyond these limits, to seek out authentic connections with those who differ in background, identity, and ideas. For those of us, as well as our students, who have not had such experiences, it is critical to expand awareness in other ways, such as reading, interviews, guest speakers, and other acts of reaching out beyond our comfort zone. For those of us teaching mostly white students, such intentional content, resources, and pedagogy are necessary in order to provide the voices and experiences our students have missed.

Being constantly aware of cultural differences, power issues, and institutional challenges may lead white faculty to "burnout" or disengage. This response is, in some ways, the ultimate power reality and example of white privilege—a white person with a secure job can decide to engage with these issues or not and choose to deny or ignore issues of power, maintaining a sense of security and privilege.

The choice to not engage, however, fails to provide a complete and enriching teaching environment for students or faculty. Educators who confront issues of race and other differences through their curriculum, pedagogy, and relationships can find deeply meaningful and rewarding experiences.

Cultural literacy and cultural humility open an avenue for faculty as effective culturally responsive educators and for primarily white institutions to more fully realize their goal of educating their students for roles in a diverse and culturally complex future.

More About the CLCI

Goals and Structure

For the past five years, groups of faculty have come together for a week in June to participate in the CLCI. This professional development opportunity began as a proposal by the Lesley University Diversity Council's Curriculum Committee to the Provost. More than forty full-time faculty/staff have gone through the program, 25 percent of the current full-time faculty.

The proposal stated that as faculty and administrators we have to do our own personal work, building our own cultural awareness and skills, as we implement curriculum and pedagogy and provide institutional support in order to create inclusive, culturally responsive environments. We wanted to encourage faculty to examine the interaction of who we are, who we teach, and what and how we teach.

The first goal for the CLCI was to establish time and resources for faculty to gather and define and identify the criteria for culturally responsive teaching in order to apply the criteria to their teaching. This required a setting and safe community for faculty to uncover and examine their beliefs, feelings, and behaviors about and toward people from diverse backgrounds. Faculty could then address the implications for curriculum and pedagogy, including developing resources to enhance social/cultural perspectives in courses and programs.

A second broad goal sought to positively affect the programs and schools of the university across the curricular and co-curricular experiences for Lesley faculty and students; to develop and expand the faculty's capacity to lead in this effort; and to solidify a community of scholars who nurture their own growth and support colleagues in their discovery and learning.

The proposal established a structure and an initial budget for a three-year pilot study. Following acceptance by the Provost, a planning team of faculty developed the specific design, including a leadership team of two faculty and the Director of Equal Opportunity and Inclusion as co-facilitators of the first-year summer experience. Faculty leadership provided modeling for participants and encouraged a collegial, equitable environment. The faculty facilitators each year represented a mix of genders, schools, and race and ethnic backgrounds, and exhibited a commitment to culturally responsive teaching, equity, and diversity.

The goal of building personal reflection and curricular/pedagogical implications was stimulated by several questions:

Who are we? What attitudes, gifts, and beliefs do we bring to our teaching?
Who are our students? What is their experience here?
What is the cultural content of our teaching/disciplines?
How do we increase culturally responsive teaching in our curriculum, pedagogy, and throughout the university culture?

A basic assumption about the pedagogy of the Institute was that a variety of materials and experiences support our learning and growth. We made use of arts, journaling, data, poetry, readings, speakers, and shared conversation in small and large groups.

The framework articulated clear student and faculty outcomes. Faculty would bring a cultural lens to their curriculum and pedagogy, and provide support to each other to extend activities for further reflection and professional practice. Students would be better prepared to be effective graduates in an increasingly global world and able to professionally act in culturally responsive ways.

Format

Each spring, all faculty received invitations to participate in the June CLCI. Outreach efforts to fill the fifteen available slots focused on creating a diverse faculty group, including race, ethnicity, gender, academic disciplines, and representation from each of the university's four schools. Adjunct faculty could attend with the support of their school Dean. Beyond the faculty, student advisors, library staff, and research staff filled out the full group of twenty participants. Each year prior participants were invited to return for the second half of the Institute, creating an ongoing community and strengthening commitments to work across programs and schools.

The opening day, following the Welcome and Introductions, participants explored a set of guidelines for how to be together during the Institute. These guidelines set a tone and expectations for our discussion, reflection, and interaction, based on respect for one another. We found the guidelines coming from the Center for Courage and Renewal especially helpful in setting this welcoming and supportive setting. (These are found in the Discussion Notes after Section III.)

Throughout the first morning, participants looked at who we are and our own experiences of difference and identity. In the afternoon we considered students' characteristics and their Lesley experiences. We also reflected on our experiences of working with diverse students in the classroom and online.

The second day we spent time in personal and small group conversation, reflecting on how we came to the work we do, and our understanding of the cultural aspects of teaching. We also explored resources with the library staff and various library guides and websites that support faculty in strengthening their curriculum and individual knowledge and skills. We began to work on a class or teaching strategy to try out in the coming year.

The third day, when past participants joined the group, two panel presentations focused our discussion: one by authors of our text, *Transforming Classroom Culture*, and another from prior participants, highlighting their specific experiences with implementing this work, including presentations from the Writing Group. The school-specific groups met in the afternoon and determined plans for the upcoming year to grow support for this work through curriculum committees, program developments, and school and faculty meetings. School groups presented their proposals on the final day to the group and the Provost. The CLCI ended with a celebratory lunch.

Assessment involved several steps. Given a journal on the first day, participants wrote and reflected in the journal throughout the Institute. Faculty filled out a daily comment sheet and a more extended questionnaire at the end of the Institute. Each school-specific group developed plans for extending CLCI into participants' curriculum and pedagogy during the academic year. In the spring of the year following the Institute, participants submitted a one-page report that discussed how the CLCI impacted their teaching, curriculum, and student outcomes during the academic year.

Through the experience of each Institute and the assessment process that the facilitators monitored, a number of changes evolved. The first year the Institute content focused on individual faculty syllabi and classroom experiences. While this has continued, successive years added a focus on a particular cultural group, such as African Americans, Indigenous peoples, or Muslims. The focus included readings, speakers, and expanded library resources. Faculty found such a focus helpful in building course resources and connections across disciplines and cultures.

We see *Culturally Responsive Teaching and Reflection in Higher Education: Promising Practices From the Cultural Literacy Curriculum Institute* as a timely, unique, and much needed book. The essays highlight the personal and teaching narratives of university faculty who are committed to culturally responsive teaching, inclusive learning environments, and building skills for responding effectively to racial and cultural difference within our academic and wider communities. We invite educators to join the discussion, individually and with colleagues.

References

Addison-Reid, B. J. (2014). *Diversity scorecard*. Cambridge, MA: Lesley University.

Brookings Institute. (2013). Shift to a majority-minority population in the U.S. happening faster than expected. Retrieved from http://www.brookings.edu/blogs/up-front/posts/2013/06/19-us-majority-minority-population-census-frey

Chavez, V. (2012). "Cultural humility: People, practices, and principles." Retrieved from https://www.youtube.com/watch?v=SaSHLbS1V4w

Dallalfar, A., Kingston-Mann, E., & Sieber, T. (Eds.). (2011). *Transforming classroom culture: Inclusive pedagogical practices*. New York, NY: Palgrave Macmillan.

European-American Collaborative Challenging Whiteness. (February 2012). White on white: Communicating about race and white privilege with critical humility. *Understanding & Dismantling Privilege, II*(I), White Privilege Conference.

Gallardo, M. E. (Ed.). (2014). *Developing cultural humility: Embracing race, privilege and power.* Los Angeles: Sage.

Gusa, D. L. (2010). White institutional presence: The impact of whiteness on campus climate. *Harvard Educational Review, 80*(4), 464–489.

Palmer, P. (2011). *Healing the heart of democracy: The courage to create a politics worthy of the human spirit.* San Francisco, CA: Jossey-Bass.

Villegas, A. M., & Lucas, T. (2002). *Educating culturally responsive teachers: A coherent approach.* New York: State University of New York Press.

Section I
Knowing Ourselves

2 Who I Am Is How I Teach

Sharlene Voogd Cochrane

One of the introductory exercises during the CLCI, "Steppingstones," invites participants to consider the events, people, or experiences that led them to their current understanding of racial awareness and their interest in culturally responsive teaching. Many of my steppingstones connected directly to the way I teach; I consider several in this essay, and the challenges and insights that guide my teaching. What are your experiences that have shaped your knowing about race and culture? How have they shaped your teaching?

Steppingstones

As a young girl growing up in Nebraska, I played the piano for the children's Sunday School worship service at the Bellevue Presbyterian Church. Young voices sang: "Jesus loves me, this I know, for the Bible tells me so," and

> Jesus loves the little children, all the children of the world;
> Red and yellow, black and white, they are precious in his sight,
> Jesus loves the little children of the world.

My sixth-grade mind made a simple assumption; if Jesus loves all the children, and they are precious, then all children should be taken care of, have equal chances, and be loved. And loving means treating people well. My mother's constant refrain, "Do unto others as you would have others do unto you," reinforced this assumption. This early experience framed my basic approach to teaching: all students are precious, and my work is to uncover and support their gifts and talents.

What I didn't know in these early years was that, although the adults taught us these songs, seemingly advocating for these values, adult actions were not always consistent with this lesson. During college, I learned about racism, systemic patterns of bias and inequality, poverty, class, and the many challenges we face as individuals and as a society in living up to that bedrock belief in the value of each person. In my personal life, as well, I would come to see the tension between songs sung and family dynamics. Recently, in reading about the lives of white anti-racist and social justice activists, I was surprised to see several mention this children's church song as formative for their earliest understanding of racial difference (Moore, Penick-Parks, & Michael, 2005).

In the fall of 1963, I enrolled at Hastings College, a small Presbyterian-related liberal arts college a three-hour train ride west from my home. The March on Washington occurred during that summer, followed in September by the bombing at the 16th St. Baptist Church. In November, President Kennedy was assassinated. At the urging of the newly installed President Johnson, Congress passed the Civil Rights Bill of 1964. After further violence during the Freedom Summer, Congress passed the Voting Rights Bill of 1965. Discussions abounded at Hastings about living out one's faith, with students wanting to know what was really happening in the South, and asking, "What is our call to action?"

In response to these questions, four of us at Hastings developed a plan for an exchange program with a black college in the South. We wanted to attend a college in the spring and support a student from that school to attend Hastings the following fall. Given the racial strife and events on the news, we decided this was the way to see for ourselves what was going on. We wrote to the Board of Higher Education of the National Presbyterian Church, which recommended Johnson C. Smith University, a historically black college in Charlotte, North Carolina.

The Dean of Students at Hastings counseled us not to go. "The South is a dangerous place, and you don't know enough about this school or the city of Charlotte."

My parents agreed, "Why would you want to do this? And you're the only girl in the group!"

My Hastings roommate worried, "There might be danger for a woman traveling there. What if you make friends there with black students, couldn't that be a problem?"

Putting the many cautions and warnings aside, in January 1965, we drove east, through Missouri and into the Appalachian Mountains of Tennessee and North Carolina. The scenery was new to all of us: long stretches of wooded countryside, narrow, curving roads, and small stores where we purchased sandwiches and soda.

Johnson C. Smith University, with a thousand students and a small seminary of forty-five students, is nestled in the hills and trees on the outskirts of

Charlotte. A wide street cut through the campus, with the original, traditional red brick buildings on one side and more recent modern dorms on the other. Founded in 1867, it was one of several historically black, church-related colleges established at the end of the Civil War. Most of the students came from North and South Carolina, although my roommate, Doris, was from Chicago. While some students questioned our presence, most took these new white students in stride, showing little reaction at all. We enrolled for a full range of classes, including religion, psychology, and literature. I joined the college choir, singing alto for Sunday chapel services.

A nearby middle school offered a tutoring program, and the one other white student and I traveled once a week, helping black students with math and English homework. As we drove back and forth to the school, Russell, the young black man driving us, repeated often, "When you get home, you need to work with white people—that's where the problems are."

For the first time I questioned what "helping" meant, and what, as a white woman, my appropriate role might be. His words have continued to remind me of the necessity for working with white students and building their cultural literacy.

As many back in Nebraska feared, especially my parents, I met a young black male student at Johnson C. Smith early in the semester and we began to date. This was new and exciting, and a bit risky, acting out, doing what I had been warned about. When I returned to Hastings for my senior year, my parents and many friends hoped this relationship would disappear.

In the summer after graduation, however, I returned to New York, and we were married in the chapel at Riverside Church. Two of his friends served as the only witnesses. No one from my family attended. My parents were upset and angrily sent me boxes of my clothes and books with a letter telling me not to come home. Moving into a tiny apartment on the upper West Side, I was in a totally new region and city, in a racially diverse neighborhood. And before long, I was pregnant with my first child.

Despite the excitement of this new life, I often felt lonely and sad. Most of my family and friends did not communicate; those who did told me that I was misguided or totally inappropriate to let my life move in this direction. I underestimated the anger, negative responses, and outright racism of my parents and others. Living out the tenets of "God loves everyone" put me in conflict with many in my church and most of my friends.

This was my first difficult and life-changing experience of the losses that often accompany crossing racial boundaries. When my son, Darin, was born, my parents' icy response began to thaw. Within a year, we traveled to Nebraska, and while the visit felt awkward and tense, at least a new connection seemed possible. Still, I carried the painful memories of this time, and felt the personal cost for many years. When students express concern about how to bring their new learning about race and racism to their families, I take their concern seriously.

Ruth Frankenberg describes a "color and power-evasive discourse" by which white people hold that skin color doesn't matter, that we are all alike. This discourse avoids any power analysis or acknowledgment of systemic racism (1993). I grew into adulthood embedded in this discourse without knowing its name. In my limited experience, it seemed all people who were proud of being white were overt racists. I didn't consider myself racist; therefore, I couldn't be white. My color-evasive stance lacked any sense of white privilege, or ability to see difference as positive; my attitudes uninformed by more comprehensive structural and cultural understanding.

Eventually my first husband and I divorced, and I married a second time when I met my soul mate, Will. We married in a family and friend celebration in the front yard of our new home in Boston. Our son Danny was born the day after Darin turned 13, followed by daughter Amy two years later, and our youngest son, William, five years later. As a white couple with a growing and integrated family, we shared a commitment to ensuring diverse experiences for our children. We chose to stay in Boston and try the public schools at a time when many white families were fleeing the city.

Our children had varying experiences of race. In a striking paradox, my bi-racial son interacted in primarily white settings, attending primarily white private schools and living in mostly white neighborhoods. My white children were often in mixed settings. All three attended the Boston Public schools, experiencing relationships, race, and ethnicity as the minority students in the classroom, with friends from many backgrounds.

An interaction with one of their teachers taught me about the confusion many teachers experience in confronting race, including my own uncomfortable moments. Visiting an art store, I noticed a package with ten skin-tone crayons, ranging from a light pinkish peach to a rich dark, dark brown. "What a neat collection for the school," I thought. "Every child's color is there!" So I purchased a package for our home, and one to give the elementary school art teacher at my children's school.

A month later, I asked the teacher, "How did the crayons work out?"

"Well, not so good," she said.
"What happened?" I asked.
"The kids all started trying to match their skin with the crayons, and comparing the color of their arms . . . it was quite unsettling, and I had to put them away."

I was completely taken aback and had no idea what to say. Like so many white people, when I didn't know what to say, I was silent. Later, questions

I didn't ask the teacher formed in my mind: What messages are we giving our children when we cannot see and celebrate the many beautiful colors they are? When we deny what is in plain sight?

Wanting to better understand how to respond and look beyond my personal experience, I signed up to participate in an anti-racism training at the Women's Theological Center, an organization holding workshops and courses about the interrelated dynamics of race, class, and religion. This two-day weekend workshop, led by two women, one black, one white, brought together a racially mixed group of about twenty people.

We usually met as one large group or racially mixed small groups, but after lunch the second day, we split up, people of color going with the black facilitator, white people with the white facilitator. These smaller, race-specific groups were to look at race and anti-racism from racially unique perspectives.

Coming back together, the black women laughed and talked engagingly with one another. One of the white women asked what happened in their group, and one of the black women said, "It's confidential."

"But how do we grow if we don't know what you are doing and saying?" the white woman insisted.

"You have your own work to do, which is separate from ours," one of the black women responded.

This continued back and forth, the white woman getting more and more tense. She couldn't accept that she was being left out of part of the black women's process. Apparently she came for learning about racism and believed this learning was dependent on the people of color teaching her.

It reminded me of the advice I received while tutoring at Johnson C. Smith in Charlotte: "When you go back home, work with white people; that's where the problems are." I have since been in settings where this dynamic is repeated. The agenda calls for a session and discussions for people of color in one room, white people in another. Coming back together can be tense, and nearly always some version of the scene above is repeated. This scenario continues to remind me that white people need to do our own work; it is not the job of people of color to teach us.

How I Teach

The same year I began my faculty position at Lesley, the Boston YWCA invited me to research the organization's history for their 125th anniversary. Excited by the prospect of pouring through original documents, I found rich resources in the archives not only about gender, but also about race. I learned that YWCA leadership supported anti-racism earlier than many similar organizations. At the National Convention in 1970, a new vision statement was approved: "One Imperative: To thrust our collective power to eliminate racism, wherever it exists and by any means necessary." In writing about the way the YWCA became integrated, I was able to interview Lucy Miller Mitchell, who became the first black board member in Boston in the late 1940s. She spoke eloquently about the realities and challenges during her years on the Board.

I learned that black women built on this vision and, beginning in the mid-1970s, established Aswalos House, a branch of the YWCA located in Roxbury, the predominantly black neighborhood in Boston, to meet the needs of women of color. Again, I was able to interview leaders of this effort. Their memories and personal accounts were critical to my understanding the goals, dynamics, and experiences of the women involved and their significant achievement.

The stories embedded in the YWCA documents and the lived experience shared in the interviews with Mitchell and the Aswalos House advocates reinforced for me the importance of learning about and listening to the narratives of those who are different from ourselves.

Even when we as white teachers strive to learn all we can and focus on our students with awareness and humility, we often have questions and times when we make mistakes or don't meet our own expectations. White teachers may find it easier to act out of our stereotypes and sense of power rather than face the challenges cultural humility requires: to remain curious and open in relationships with those who are different.

Several years ago, I was mentoring a black male student who was writing a final thesis. He found it difficult to find time to develop his thoughts and do the writing, having, like many of our students, a full-time job and a family. In order to help him, I gave him several extensions, trying to understand and be flexible. A year passed, with us setting deadlines, and him heading off to do his writing for a month or so and then not meeting the deadline. In a Diversity Council meeting considering the retention of black students, we discussed ways white teachers can fail black students. Was I in fact thinking my student would never be able to finish his work? I was certainly prolonging the process with no specific support. I had to face my own stereotypical response of not expecting enough from my student. The next time we met, we set up weekly conferences, with short, specific parts of the thesis to write. He gained momentum and within the next semester he completed a fine thesis and graduated.

I teach predominantly white students and continue to search for ways to meet the challenges involved. Students vary widely in their knowledge, experiences, and attitudes about race, gender, and religion. They may not have questioned their own racial experiences, and many hold a color-blind stance. I remember how long it has taken me to grow into valuing myself as a white woman, and I welcome the students wherever they are in their journey. Students that have a more nuanced understanding still have much to learn. As the concept of cultural humility reminds us, responding to race, difference, or others requires lifelong learning.

My course "Seminar in U.S. History: Intersections of Race, Gender, and Religion" represents one such learning experience. The syllabus follows the process that has been significant for my own learning, especially critical reflection about students' experiences and careful listening and learning about the experiences of others. Students read and discuss works by and about women—white, black, Native American, Christian, Jewish, Muslim—living at various periods of U.S. history. They interrogate their own life and the lives of others in terms of race, gender, and religion, through exercises, projects, and research. The goal is a classroom space where students can move from fear and uneasiness to understanding and action.

In the "Family Timeline" assignment, students consider three generations of the women in their family (or other friends or relatives) and place them on the course timeline, in terms of their experience of gender, race, and religion. What was happening to women in their family when the Civil War took place? How was their family impacted by the early twentieth century black migration to the north, the Great Depression, World War II? What kinds of work, relationships, and stories do they uncover? Displaying this information visually, students create charts, timelines, mobiles, quilts, and collages of what race, gender, and religion look like for their family.

The white students generally respond positively to the course, though some experience great dissonance as they discover the mixed messages they have received about race and the realities of social and structural racism and privilege within which they live. In their final reflective paper, they talk about their reactions to the course.

Comments from white students often include statements such as:

> As a white woman, I never really thought about how any other person thought. I thought all people had the same experiences I did. Boy was I wrong. I had no idea the racism and hatred many people face everyday . . . I know that when I am the most defensive, I have the most to learn.

Students of color also express value for the course, for different reasons:

> This class helped me strengthen my position as a Black woman with a positive self-image. I will continue to pass my pride to my children and to the children I teach.

Another was pleased to find that the readings,

> especially the ones on privilege, made my classmates realize the priv-
> ilege of being white . . . This was the most powerful learning to me
> because all of my experiences in classes that had similar themes con-
> sisted mainly of a constant denial of ever having any kind of privilege
> over someone of color.

As students sought to share their new attitudes and knowledge with others, they began to consider what they could do next, though they worried about how to do that. In addition to reading more African American history, one student said, tentatively,

> I will risk ridicule and criticism to make my opinion and voice heard.
> I will become a more active listener . . . I will not be a co-conspirator by
> remaining indifferent or by keeping silent.

Another student was determined to

> use a voice that is not shrill with accusation . . . I try, on a daily basis, to
> find ways to teach about race, class and gender discrimination in ways
> that do not intimidate.

A small number of students reflected aloud that they felt anger, shame, or confusion, often the collision between their home environment and this new information. One student expressed embarrassment within the class:

> [I] shared my answer with the class but felt ashamed admitting this
> ignorance. I left class totally disheartened. I actually got into my car
> and burst into tears, though I was not completely sure why I was
> crying.

By the end of class she expressed satisfaction with her learning in the class, but was still concerned about a lack of support for herself outside the class-room: "How does one person make a stab at changing while still maintaining a family that may not support these efforts?"

Having found such a lack of support in my own family and how difficult it was for me to speak out, even to my children's art teacher, I appreciated her honesty and her anxiety.

Like this student, others may feel uncomfortable talking about these new ideas or become guilty or angry as they learn about the history and their own family stories.

I offer the concept of "white allies," as described by Beverly Tatum, to provide a new role for consciously aware white people: those joining the efforts for social justice and moving beyond paralyzing guilt and shame toward positive action. Tatum found that most of her white students had only three models of whiteness: white supremacist, color- and power-blind, and "guilty white," where their shame and guilt became immobilizing. She presents another model: those white people who have "resisted the role of oppressor and who have been allies to people of color" (1994, p. 471). Though they are often unknown and unrecognized, their stories can be uncovered and serve as a model for current white students struggling with their own white identity. Reading Tatum's work brought new ideas to our conversations, and hope and possibility to many of the students.

Learning about racism and its intersections with gender and religion is never complete. Yet, as these students show, once they have a way to read, talk, and explore their own realities, they grow in important ways. The course reinforces for me how hungry students are to have a safe place to explore these issues, talk to others, and (for white students) to build their own positive white identity, where they can act as allies or speak up when faced with racist language or ideas. As faculty, we need to do our own work, and then find ways to make spaces available for students to do theirs.

My background, my experiences at Lesley, the stories I hear from colleagues of color, and my parenting of both white and mixed race children continue to challenge my understanding of racism in our country and communities. Concepts such as racial identity formation, power and privilege, systemic racism, and social justice name a new complexity to what had once been a simple color-blind belief. We may all be children of God, but racially embedded structures, fears, and policies continue to limit and challenge equality for all.

Individuals need continuing efforts to learn about and challenge racism. I have a broader understanding of race and my own white identity now than I did in Bellevue, or at Johnson C. Smith, or when I raised my children. Yet, there is always more to learn, more layers to unpeel of my own racism, blind spots, and privilege. The concept of cultural humility encourages me with its call to lifelong learning, acknowledging and interrupting powerful systems, and linking individual action and institutional support to increase racial and social justice.

My friend Donna Bivens, a retreat co-facilitator and wise black woman, has written about what white people and people of color need to do in supporting one another:

> In homogeneous settings, white people can help each other to understand
> white privilege and to challenge each other to truly accept the leadership

of, and to equitably share benefit and ownership with, people of color. . . .
In heterogeneous settings, all must make sure that systemic racism, white
privilege and internalized racism are understood and addressed. We can
then work to build inclusive and intercultural cultures that refuse to accept
racial disparity and that bravely expose the lies of race and racism

(2005, p. 50)

I have been fortunate in my journey to have friends, white and people of
color, who support my learning and growth, and who challenge me when
I fall back on old habits, incomplete understanding, and privileged "unknow-
ing." These relationships happen when we "do unto others as we would have
them do unto us" on an interpersonal level, and when we acknowledge and
work to interrupt the social and economic realities that plague race relationships and equity in our society; when the person I am and actions I take with
humility and courage reinforce one another.

Questions for Reflection

1. Use the "Steppingstones in Responding to Difference" exercise in the
    Reflections section to reflect on what events or people, both positive and
    negative, have influenced your perspectives about race and difference.
    What do you learn? What surprises do you find? How have your gifts as
    a teacher been supported?
2. Create a timeline of three generations of women in your family, filling
    in what you can about race, religion, and gender. What patterns do you
    discover? What information is new to you? What messages have you
    inherited from these experiences?
3. What parts of yourself do you bring to your teaching? What have you
    learned about race, gender, and religion that shapes how you teach?

References

Bivens, D. (2005). What is internalized racism? In MP Associates, Inc. and the Center
    for Assessment and Policy Development (Eds.), *Flipping the script: White privi-
    lege and community building* (pp. 43–51). Boston: MP Associates.
Frankenberg, R. (1993). *White women, race matters: The social construction of
    whiteness*. Minneapolis: University of Minnesota Press.
Moore, E., Penick-Parks, M. W., & Michael, A. (Eds.). (2015). *Everyday white people
    confront racial and social injustice: 15 stories*. Sterling, VA: Stylus.
Tatum, B. D. (1994, Summer). Teaching white students about racism: The search for
    white allies and the restoration of hope. *Teachers College Record, 95*(4), 462–476.

3 Reflections on Identity and Privilege

Julie A. Stanwood

Introduction

I am a middle-aged, able-bodied, heterosexual white woman, and I currently serve as a full-time administrator for Lesley University and as an adjunct instructor for Lesley and other local colleges. I had lived decades without thinking much about my cultural identity or that of folks around me, until I attended the Lesley University Cultural Literacy Curriculum Institute the summer of 2014. There I learned how much I do not know about multicultural concerns and power imbalances in our society. The level of my ignorance hit hard and encouraged me to actively engage the process of enhancing my own understanding of what it means to be culturally aware. I realized it would be necessary to explore and reflect on my own identity and privilege in order to effectively provide optimal educational services to a diverse student population. I am hopeful such exploration will lead to cultural awareness and advocacy for social justice, though the space between acknowledging the issues and my action can feel immense.

Privilege and Challenges

I spent most of my childhood in an affluent town in northeast Massachusetts. The town's population was mainly white, and the majority of my cultural influences came from my Swedish grandparents. A "good Swede" was expected to worship God on Sundays and work hard for one's family, with the understanding that one could achieve anything if one worked hard enough. I was told to never accept handouts, and there was a pervasive, unspoken message to always avoid expressing negative emotions.

My father owned a family florist business and spent much of his time and energy managing it. My mother attended college evenings, where she earned undergraduate and graduate degrees. One of her first professional roles was that of a psychiatric nurse at Danvers State Mental Hospital. She truly cared about people who suffered from mental illness. While she moved around to several regional mental health institutions, she retained passion for the state institutions and protested their closings throughout the 1970s and '80s. For my mother, action for social justice took the form of discourse around societal responsibility to care for the mentally ill. I was not exposed to oppression beyond my mother's passion and the abstract concepts I heard about in history classes.

As a shy, quiet child, I loved to read. I carried books everywhere and would find a corner in which to sit and read whenever possible. I did not know I was probably being rude, but the ability to tune out the world served as protection from the unpleasant aspects of my life. At that time, I would have laughed if someone had told me about my white privilege because my family would be considered lower middle class in any town as wealthy as the one of my childhood. My mother and father did not have the income that my peer's parents had and were not able to buy me the objects that were considered status symbols. In retrospect, I understand my family was not poor, but rather, a typical white middle-class family. There was always food in the refrigerator and we had cars, a television, and bicycles, with safe, open places for riding.

The only person of color I knew was the boy who sat near me in homeroom. He was the son of a famous professional sports figure, and he hung out with the school jocks. I never wondered how difficult it must have been for him to be the only person of color in our town's single high school. He must have felt lonely, but at the time, I did not give him a second thought. One of the most fundamental assumptions of white privilege is the expectation that we can perform daily life functions among people of our own race (McIntosh, 1990). I simply assumed his world was perfect because of his financial status.

My loathing of the school years likely led to me becoming pregnant at age sixteen. My parents were displeased, to say the least. Given the choice of abortion or exile, I chose the latter. My boyfriend (now husband) and I dropped out of school, and I lived with a friend until he found a full-time job. His brother worked for a large yogurt company and pulled strings to get my husband a position in the warehouse. We found an apartment in an old mill town nearby, and I went to the free clinic to get prenatal care. I was one of the few white women at the clinic. The physicians there performed their pro bono obligations and talked to each other while we (clients) laid on examining tables separated by thin curtains. The doctors behaved as if women of a certain socioeconomic status were not smart enough to discuss healthcare. I remember the rage I experienced, listening to my obstetrician discuss my condition with his peers as if I was not there. That was my first brief lens into what life might be like to not be a person of privilege.

After my son was born, I took the high school equivalency test and, like my mother, attended college nights while working days. My grandmother contacted me and facilitated a reconciliation with my family. I worked for my father's business and completed my undergraduate degree in business administration. I applied for an accounting position at a college in Boston, and at that point my cloistered view of the world changed markedly. I met different kinds of people who shared varieties of life experiences to which I had never been exposed: people who identified as non-heterosexual, people with disabilities, people of color, of non-Christian religions, and more. I witnessed the practicalities of how people with disabilities could not enter certain non-accessible buildings on campus and, on an intellectual level, I understood that injustice was, in fact, still prevalent in the twentieth century. I did not consider myself part of that system of oppression, however, as I believed that role to be the white man's purview. Goodman (2011) suggested people tend to associate with the subordinate parts of their identities, and this tendency to hide one's privilege is an effective means by which to deny it.

Awareness and Professional Growth

I discovered I had a passion for higher education as well as inherent counseling skills, and I wanted my work with college students to be meaningful. I took advantage of my employment at a higher education institution and earned a graduate degree in counseling, supporting a career shift from tuition collector to academic advisor. My counseling program required students to investigate concepts of privilege in a course called "Power, Privilege, and Oppression." I heard the words and easily passed the class, but again, did not believe myself to be a person of privilege. Boysen and Vogel (2008) discovered that while white counseling students are able to learn ideas and incorporate multicultural training to their growing repertoires of skills, implicit racial biases often remain beneath consciousness. Unless these ideas are mined and discussed in an open and honest fashion, racism remains prevalent, even in the educational environment (Sue, 2005).

My first real insight into the depth of my privilege happened in Mexico, where I have served as chaperone to a photography class that has been offered every year on and off since 2007.

My own experience through life had effectively illustrated one of the key family values I had learned as a child, that if one works hard enough, one could achieve a place among the middle class. In a Mexican village, however, hard work does not lead to anything beyond another day of hard work. In the Mexican village where the photography course took place, the women work all day. Some families live in shelters constructed of corrugated tin walls, dirt floors, and no plumbing. The women have to wash dishes and clothes by hand and then go off to work in whatever form that takes.

The Lesley University students in the photography course spend their days with the Mexican families my colleague has known for decades. My colleague, *la profesora*, is a professional photographer. Many years ago *la profesora* befriended a village woman and became part of a Mexican family. The family members appointed her the role of godmother to Paola, one of the children. *La profesora* has lived with the family at times and has contributed to the family's welfare in the form of financial gifts. *La profesora* paid for Paola's uncle to attend medical school. Despite consistent financial contributions, family members live much the same way today as they did when *la profesora* first entered their lives. In this village, if one is not born in wealth, one will not attain wealth. This is the place where I really understood, albeit as an observer, that the world is not fair.

There are people in the Mexican villages that hate white people. Many times I walked down the streets with students, and residents slammed their doors yelling profanities. I was initially stunned by such hostility. *What did I do?* was my first reaction. Now I almost embrace the hostility; if I were in the same situation, I would likely feel the way these residents do. The contempt I hold for spoiled American celebrities might be akin to how the Mexicans feel about me. What did I do for these people? Absolutely nothing.

One year, a man we met in the city, Hilario, invited members of the photography class to visit his village. His family members were weavers, and his father showed us how the rugs are made, how the wool is dyed using plants, and so on. In a cringe-worthy memory, I engaged in a dialogue with one of Hilario's brothers. He accused me of being a rich, privileged, white American. I believed this accusation to be insulting and not applicable to me. I told him that I do not truly possess anything, that the bank owns my home, my car, my furniture, and my student loans. Imagine the arrogance of this: complaining about my debt to someone who would unlikely ever have access to a bank loan, to higher education. Sue, Bingham, Porche-Burke, and Vasquez (1999) suggested white privilege is often invisible to white people because certain advantages are simply always available to them. White people are therefore unable to perceive the existence of such advantages.

Over the years, I have had the pleasure of watching Paola grow. On a recent trip, I remember sitting with Paola in the back of a pick-up truck, speeding down the highway. Paola, at age sixteen, was talking about how much she would like to visit me in the U.S. I told her I would be thrilled to host her visit, though I wondered if this would ever be possible, even with *la profesora* in her life. Paola started stroking my skin and said she wished her skin were like mine. "Why do you want nasty, wrinkled old-lady skin?" I asked her, touching her arm, "Your skin is beautiful." This is not what she meant and I knew it. I didn't have the vocabulary to discuss it, certainly not in Spanish and maybe not in English. What could I say? The exchange was not authentic.

The incident did give me an opportunity to think about the power of skin color in a way I had never considered. Even during our struggles of being teens-on-our-own-with-a-baby, my husband and I experienced the privileges of being white; my husband's ability to procure a steady job (despite limited education), the guarantee our apartment-residence applications would always be accepted, and my predisposition to academic success was, no doubt, a result of having attended an affluent public school system. These advantages are among the privileges I, as a white woman, have been privy to even through my life's greatest challenges. McIntosh (1990) referred to this reflective process as unpacking the invisible knapsack of white privilege. In owning the benefits I have enjoyed throughout my life, I must also admit the system disadvantages others, right here in my country. I do not need to be in Mexico to witness oppression.

Today I still have the ability to close out the world around me. I hear other women my age complain about being invisible: nobody is more invisible than a middle-aged woman, they say. Is this phenomenon specific to middle-aged white women? I suspect it is. A few years back, I was in Washington DC attending a conference. While I jogged across the lawn of the White House, I heard helicopters and noticed security people running around installing gates, herding people away. I almost bumped into a male security guard. He assessed me from head to toe, rolled his eyes, and waved me along, inside the secure area. I understand now this was a result of my whiteness (and likely my gender). For the most part, being invisible suited me just fine, but knowing it is a privilege associated with my race makes it feel like an underhanded trick. Being invisible also does not afford me opportunities to connect with others, to take risks, and to contribute to the world in a meaningful way.

At the time of this narrative, the option to become involved in cultural consciousness efforts has become increasingly important; one might even consider it an urgent mandate. Recent events in the United States, including the deaths of young black men at the hands of law enforcement, have encouraged angry protests from college students across the country. Students at my institution visited a meeting of the Board of Trustees and declared university members do not adequately address racial and multicultural issues, that such topics are not recognized in the classroom, and that faculty are unwilling to engage in honest dialogue.

In a survey of white faculty members Sue and colleagues (2009) hoped to learn how faculty members perceived and managed classroom dialogues on race. The researchers discovered anxiety was one emotion prevalent among white faculty. The participants reported they might lose control of the class, could be perceived as racist by the students, and felt they did not possess the expertise to negotiate such discussions. It appears members of my institution, no matter how thoughtful and aware of diversity issues, are not immune to similar uncertainties. Given the current tensions and demand for culturally responsive behaviors, I feel that now is the time to take risks and discuss racial issues in multiple higher education forums.

Action Project

My primary responsibility to the institution is to administer effective academic advising practices to visual art students. In researching best practices for multicultural advising, I discovered there is no handbook with easy-to-follow instructions. In fact, there are many opportunities for misstep. Harding (2012) suggested advisors must be careful to avoid stereotyping and that ethnic groups have varieties of attitudes around seeking and receiving assistance. While there are some commonalities associated with low socio-economic status among black and Hispanic populations, one cannot make assumptions. Students of color bring unique experiences and backgrounds to their institutions; as Museus and Ravello (2010) noted, there is much diversity within minority groups, and each student is a complex individual. These points are important as they underscore the challenges that emerge for developing effective strategies to serve a multicultural student population.

Much information has been documented about the millennial generation—college students born in the period 1982–2002 (Coomes & DeBard, 2004)—and that this population possesses certain characteristics such as being special, sheltered, confident, conventional, achieving, and pressured with regard to expectations of achievement in multiple disciplines. Many campus personnel members, myself included, have utilized millennial research to serve students, without considering that such research is based on white student demographics and experiences. The traits named above may not be necessarily applicable to college students of color born during the same period. Marbley, Hull, Polydore, Bonner, and Burley (2007) proposed that many African American children were unlikely to have had access to the same resources as white children, and that the needs of this student population may therefore differ greatly from that of their white peers (Henry, Butler, & West, 2011).

Harding (2012) suggested obtaining cultural awareness is not enough to influence transformative change. The advisor must gain cultural competence, a combination of knowledge, skills, and actions that serve to enhance the college experience for students of color. The culturally competent advisor must also examine her own background, cultural history, baggage, and general understanding of her place in the community. I would like to take this perspective further in my work with students, however, and strive to gain cultural humility. Tervalon and Murray-Garcia (1998) described cultural humility as requiring not only sensitivity to privilege and power within a narrow, situation-specific field, but a lifelong reflection and attention to how one's position in the world might oppress others. Cultural humility requires one to consider people and institutional structures in a relentless pursuit to destroy unfair advantages and develop systems of equity.

An unexpected opportunity for me to start practicing what I had learned from my identity exploration occurred during the spring semester of 2015. The University Provost had invited schools to respond to recent injustices that had been occurring across the country. I was determined to mobilize the peer mentors, the school's student leaders, to develop a visual art project that would involve the entire university community and bring attention to the national deterioration of racial relations. I did not know what to do or how to start, and felt extreme discomfort in introducing the topic to the students. How would I possibly achieve cultural humility if I could not even discuss it with others? I had one semester to make something happen, and there was no time for apprehension.

I asked the students to read and critique the essay, *Unpacking the Invisible Knapsack* (McIntosh, 1990). My co-instructor and I were gratefully surprised by the students' comments and passion around the subject. While there were only three nonwhite students among the sixteen, all members seemed knowledgeable of injustice issues and eager to engage in some type of activism. They showed none of the fear I had experienced in discussing racial tensions, and I was simultaneously relieved and ashamed of my own trepidation.

One of the students proposed the idea of using wheat paste (a liquid adhesive similar to decoupage) to affix images to the public sidewalks in front campus buildings. The images would comprise photos of signs and other depictions of protests and civil rights movements from past decades through the present. Students would conduct research to cull the images and invite community members to submit images as well. The students would then impose the pastings to the sidewalks late at night to make a big splash for people walking down the road the next day. The wheat paste would deteriorate with weather and the messages would also fade with the images. Photography students would document public reaction to the images and the deterioration of the messages from the sidewalk. The students titled the project "How long will this last?" and it was meant to evoke thought around social injustice and America's unfortunate inability to eradicate racial inequalities. The students would create buttons and flyers and had grand ideas as to the project's culmination, with an opening exhibition and a community dialogue about the project. My co-instructor was an artist, knew how to use wheat paste, and was eager to lead the effort. It seemed as if nothing could go wrong.

I would like to report that the project was a huge success. In retrospect I think of it as a truly innovative concept that went completely unrecognized by the university community. While the students initially seemed so comfortable holding discourse around a difficult topic, there were moments of panic and anxiety throughout the semester. The students questioned their abilities to achieve the intended outcomes, and the white students did not feel they had the right to engage in such activities. I was not yet comfortable enough with my own skills in leading a racial injustice project to effectively serve as a calming influence. Other students were busy with a number of academic pressures and lost motivation. My colleague discovered the City of Cambridge does not welcome Guerilla art installation in any public spaces, and students had to get permissions from administration to do the project on school property, thus eliminating the "splash." Administrative members were uneasy about the esthetics of the project, despite its theme, causing students to question the integrity of the Provost's request for speaking out.

After weeks of agonizing over details, the images were imposed to the walkway in front of the art building. One of the students photographed a passerby pointing to one of the images while speaking with her child. This was a highlight; for the most part, few people seemed to understand or care about the project. On the third day after pasting, one of the university maintenance workers scraped and washed all the images away because the rain/paste combination made them slippery. There was no opening exhibition, and only three people showed up to attend the community dialogue.

Conclusion

I have no regrets about attempting this project despite its failure to garner public attention. While others would not have labeled this activity risky, my own level of introversion and discomfort in creating controversy rendered it as such for me, and it was a step, albeit tiny, to responding to a social justice issue. It also made me realize my path to gaining cultural humility will not be easy, nor will it offer a how-to manual. The reflection of my history and developing awareness of oppressive systems serves to keep me out of my hiding place, and the mission ahead contains all of the political, complicated, messy, and uncomfortable elements I have spent my life trying to avoid. It is still a fact I am far from having earned the title of activist, but the uneasy feelings I experience during missed opportunities serves to remind me of the challenges and potential for growth throughout the process.

Questions for Reflection

1. What is an experience you've had that indicates your racial privilege, or lack of privilege? How do your childhood experiences influence your identity in terms of power and privilege?
2. What steps could you take to build your cultural consciousness?
3. How might you begin to take (even the smallest) steps to changing oppressive systems? To increase the cultural literacy of your students?

References

Boysen, G. A., & Vogel, D. L. (2008). The relationship between levels of training, implicit bias, and multicultural competency among counselor trainees. *Training and Education in Professional Psychology, 2*(2), 103–110.

Coomes, M., & DeBard, R. (Eds.). (2004). *Serving the millennial generation*. San Francisco, CA: Jossey-Bass.

Goodman, D. J. (2011). *Promoting diversity and social justice: Educating people from privileged groups*. New York, NY: Routledge.

Harding, B. (2012). Advising students of color. *NACADA Clearinghouse of Academic Advising Resources*. Retrieved from http://www.nacada.ksu.edu/Resources/ Clearinghouse/View-Articles/Advising-students-of-color.aspx

Henry, W., Butler, D., & West, N. (2011). Things are not as rosy as they seem: Psychosocial issues of contemporary black college women. *Journal of College Student Retention, 13*(2), 137–153.

Marbley, A. F., Hull, W., Polydore, C. L., Bonner, F. A., & Burley, H. (2007). African American millennial college students: Owning the technological middle passage. *National Association of Student Affairs Professionals, 10*(1), 7–19.

McIntosh, P. (1990). White privilege: Unpacking the invisible knapsack. *Independent School, 49*(2), 31.

Museus, S., & Ravello, J. (2010). Characteristics of academic advising that contribute to racial and ethnic minority student success at predominately white institutions. *The Journal of National Academic Advising Association, 30*(1), 47–58.

Sue, D. W. (2005). Racism and the conspiracy of silence: Presidential address. *The Counseling Psychologist, 33*(1), 100–114.

Sue, D. W., Bingham, R., Porche-Burke, L., & Vasquez, M. (1999). The diversification of psychology: A multicultural revolution. *American Psychologist, 54*(12), 1061–1069.

Sue, D. W., Torino, G. C., Capodilupo, C. M., Rivera, D. P., & Lin, A. I. (2009). How white faculty perceive and react to difficult dialogues on race. *The Counseling Psychologist, 37*(8), 1090–1115.

Tervalon, M., & Murray-Garcia, J. (1998). Cultural humility versus cultural competence: A critical distinction in defining physician training outcomes in multicultural education. *Journal of Health Care for the Poor and Underserved, 9*(2), 117–125.

4   Embracing My Social Class Transition

A Journey to More Effective Teaching

Michaela Kirby

If I belong here, will I lose my roots?
If I belong here, will I cease to have my connection to and with my family?
If I belong here, am I a traitor to my upbringing?
If I belong here, am I rejecting all that I hold dear?
If I belong here, am I devaluing parts of myself?
If I belong here, can I still be all of who I am?

—M. Kirby

Introduction

As a new professor teaching about social class in a multicultural master's level course in 1999, I used an experiential exercise suggested by a colleague in which students place themselves in a line in relation to each other based on the financial resources of their family of origin. This exercise required that they speak to each other about their level of wealth to determine their relative position on the line. Once everyone had found their "place" on the line, people asked questions of those from different financial statuses. The discussion during this exercise became affectively charged, especially around anger experienced by working-class and lower socioeconomic status students. I found it difficult to manage the affect in a way that ensured productive learning.

Several years later, when I taught the multicultural course again, I tried a different approach to teaching about social class. The students read *Where We Stand: Class Matters* by bell hooks (2000) as a point of reference for reflecting on their own class background. When we reviewed this assignment in the classroom, the discussion remained intellectual and distanced in contrast to that first experience with the strong affective response. This distance limited the effectiveness in truly learning about the impact of class and socioeconomic status on people's life opportunities.

At the time of the first teaching experience, I had recently graduated from a doctoral program, was deeply in debt with student loans, and struggling to survive financially as a single parent in an expensive city. I felt confused knowing I was privileged because of my race, education, and teaching position, while simultaneously living the stressful reality of financial struggle. My classroom seemed filled with strong emotion around social class differences. By the second teaching experience, my economic situation had changed drastically because I had a partner with more financial resources. I felt incredible relief and gratitude, but I also felt guilty that I had not solved these problems with my own hands. I kept a distance from these difficult feelings, and, interestingly, my class during this second teaching experience also kept a distance, remaining in a very intellectual place. Through the training I attended at the Cultural Literacy Curriculum Institute (CLCI) and further reading about social class transitions, I have come to believe that my personal history as well as circumstances at the time influenced my choices and had the potential to either limit or amplify the effectiveness of my teaching.

An important part of my personal history involved transitioning from "first generation to go to college" to becoming a professor, a significant social, economic, and cultural leap. This transition for students who are the first in their family to attend college is now being named, recognized, and supported on college campuses. Colleges have established programs for "first gen" students recognizing the stress of the distance that these students feel between home and school (Pappano, 2015). For me, this transition to college left a schism in my sense of identity, which I did not recognize as being about social class until I read Zandy's book, *Liberating Memory: Our Work and Our Working Class Consciousness*, a collection of writings of first-generation college attendees who became college professors. Zandy points out, "According to the book of success, a working-class identity is intended for disposal. In order to 'make it' into the dominant society, one 'overcomes' the class circumstances of birth, and moves into the middle and then upper class" (Zandy, 1995, p. 1). The message is that you have to "give up" where you have been and "take on" the values of the higher social class. This process of overcoming working-class roots produces "class amnesia," where people lose touch with their working-class experiences. But as Zandy (1995) so eloquently states:

> Memory has a purpose. It is a bridge between the subjective and the intersubjective—the private and unprivileged circumstances of individual lives—and the objective—the collective history of class oppression. It is a way of moving from personal pain to public and cultural work. The 'stuff' of one's life can be transformed into fruitful practices.
>
> (p. 4)

Through the experience of the CLCI sessions and the Writing Group that followed, I became aware that I needed to recover from my own working-class amnesia in order to make use of my working-class identity and consciousness to strengthen my teaching. I had to understand the impact of social class and class transition in my life in order to be a more effective teacher.

If I Belong Here, Will I Lose My Roots?

As I was growing up, there was no question that I was going to college. My mother, for whom college was out of reach, was very clear that all three of her daughters were going to get a bachelor's degree. As a "first gen" student, I experienced difficulties right from the beginning. With no idea how to choose a college, even applying was a hit or miss process. In the end, decisions were based mainly on driving distance, as I wanted to be away, but it had to be close enough that my parents could drive to the school and back home on the same day.

When my parents dropped me off that first day in September 1976, I was seeing the campus for the first time, as I had not known that people visited colleges before enrolling. The first meeting with my roommate is still a vivid memory. She had asked me what my parents did for work—one of her parents was a stockbroker and the other a dentist. At that moment, the fact that my parents had not gone to college registered with me in a completely different way. I had known this all of my life, but it was not unusual in my working-class neighborhood. But, in this moment, this fact was reflected back to me as difference laden with judgment and shame. It mirrored the difference of the "equipment" that each of us brought to our college dorm room; I brought a hot pot and a radio, she brought a refrigerator and full stereo. I discovered over time that the college I attended was a highly competitive college, a "back up" school for students who applied to Ivy League schools. I had no awareness of the status of this university and did not know what "Ivy League" meant.

For the first time in my life I struggled academically that first semester. One course, *Problems of Philosophy*, was appropriately titled, as my parochial high school education had not prepared me for debating questions such as determinism and indeterminism. I kept wondering which was the "correct" answer. Feeling lost and desperate, I went to talk with the professor who had followed in his father's footsteps of doctoral study and faculty appointment at an elite private school. He authored the textbook we were using and he had no capacity or frame of reference for understanding my struggles and me. We were from two radically different cultural contexts. From my family background and education, I had no idea how to think critically and engage in the intellectual debate of ideas that he required in the class assignments.

I do not think he understood the depth of my confusion. Despite sharing the English language, we could not communicate across what was an invisible, unrecognized divide.

The social environment was no easier. Social life centered on fraternities and sororities, an unknown and unappealing prospect for me. Joining a sorority would not have been possible given the financial requirements, but I was not drawn to these social groups, feeling out of place and awkward.

The next year I transferred to a small women's college where I had an amazingly different experience. In this environment, I was able to find my voice, engage in a wide range of experiences, and discover my strengths and abilities. It was not until ten years later during my doctoral program, while talking with a friend who was also first generation going to college, that I realized for the first time that my discomfort at the first college was about social class.

If I Belong Here, Am I a Traitor to My Upbringing?

When I decided to go back to school to get a master's degree in Expressive Therapies, my family was a bit surprised. Wasn't I done? I had my degree. When I graduated from my master's program, my father sent a graduation card with a note saying, "Hope it's the last time," so choosing to pursue a doctoral degree was an even more difficult decision. I worried that a doctoral degree would create too large a chasm between my world and the world of my family of origin. The difference and distance from my family was poignant and growing wider. Completing a doctorate felt like crossing an invisible line from which there was no return—an unbridgeable gap. Barbara Jensen (2012) reflects my own feelings eloquently in her book, *Reading Classes: On Culture and Classism in America*: "I wanted middle class skills and knowledge, but I was afraid that if I strayed too far, I would never again feel I belonged in my loving extended family. Worse, I felt that I would somehow betray them" (p. 54). Tears came to my eyes as I read these words, as it so closely paralleled my feelings about my struggle around advanced study.

If I Belong Here, Am I Rejecting All That I Hold Dear?

Based on Jensen's (2012) research, there are some specific differences in cultural values between middle-class and working-class cultures. Middle- and upper-class families focus on and value individuality; they celebrate competition, individual success, and achievement. Children are encouraged to develop their abilities and to achieve success, for example to excel academically and achieve recognition and awards. This is not the same for working-class groups. Belonging and being part of the group supersedes individual achievement in terms of importance for many working-class people. The values are on: "caring connections with others within the group, communal values of sharing and helping, trust of feelings and personal stories, loyalty and family-like bonds with others" (Jensen, 2012, p. 62). The sense of "belonging" also has differences across class. Middle-class people are able to negotiate and be comfortable finding a sense of belonging within as well as across "established hierarchies of power." But for working-class people, they look for a sense of belonging with peers (Jensen, 2012).

As I reflect on my background, I can see these working-class values at play. In my family, my academic success was acknowledged and recognized as a "good" thing, but it was not celebrated or shared with the extended family or friends. My sisters and I all had different strengths, and, if anything, the ability to sing at family gatherings was more highly valued in my family than academic success. I have come to recognize that I, unconsciously, have prioritized belonging and contributing to my department— as I would in my family—over achieving my own individual success and promotion.

For the majority of my higher education career, I have been in faculty positions where I teach as well as carry administrative responsibilities. I have strengths in organizing systems. I see this as helping "the rubber hit the road" so that my department can run more smoothly and effectively. I have come to recognize that taking on administrative responsibility is a way that I have lived out my working-class values of sharing and helping. It has been my way to feel part of the department and a sense of connection to the group. This way of contributing is much more familiar and comfortable for me than the individual achievement of academic scholarship and publication. When a fellow faculty member suggested that I needed to spend less time giving feedback to my students on their papers in order to focus on my own writing and publishing, I was appalled. It was anathema to my beliefs about my role.

I have come to see that I am still functioning in a working-class mindset in the midst of my faculty position. My focus and time is spent on teaching and time-consuming administrative tasks while failing to focus on my own scholarship, publications, and rank advancement. As I spoke about this with a friend, I became tearful as I realized that I am still trying to "fit" in my family of origin by holding onto my working-class identity in how I navigate my faculty position. I do not want to forget who I am, to lose the values and skills I received growing up, nor my sense of connection to these roots. I want to recognize the rich environment of my youth and to find a way to honor my background by bringing these values and capacities into a respected placed in this academic world.

If I Belong Here, Am I Devaluing Parts of Myself?

When I began working with the CLCI Writing Group and decided to focus on my teaching about social class, I had no idea this would take me straight into the heart of my current struggle in my academic position: my struggle with writing for publication. This seems to be a lynchpin for me—marking the place of conflict between my working-class roots and my professional academic identity. Very early on in my doctoral program, when I was struggling to write my first paper, I had a dream. In the dream, I was at the school attending classes when an administrator approached me, said there had been a mistake as I was not supposed to be accepted into the program, and that I would have to leave. In the dream, I was devastated and sobbing, questioning whether I really had to leave and heartbroken at losing this opportunity. Following this dream, I was finally able to successfully complete my first paper. The dream seemed to give a creative outlet for the self-doubts and anxiety that I carried with me about my own scholarly abilities that were interfering with my ability to complete that first writing assignment in my doctoral program. "Did I really belong here?" seemed to be an active question for me on an unconscious level.

Over the years, I have worked on several pieces for publication. Often, when I would carve out a bit of writing time in the midst of my other academic responsibilities, I would feel as if my mind "shattered" as I tried to focus on the work. I questioned and doubted everything I wrote and could not successfully organize and complete any written piece. I believe this was my struggle with the imposter syndrome, "the feeling that one has fooled people to be successful and the fear that one will be 'found out'" (Jensen, 2012, p. 163). My internal critic was wreaking havoc, warning me that writing would expose me as the fraud that I was and that I would lose the status I had achieved. In contrast, I could present at conferences with ease because I could make a connection with the audience by using the social skills I have from my working-class roots. Verbal presentations are also transient, but the written word—a published article—felt like a very different level of exposure and risk for me.

I experienced my lack of publishing as my own personal failing, until I began to explore the literature around social class and the issues of crossing class. Jensen (2012) says:

> These reactions to higher education are *not* a result of personal failings but of cultural clash and domination. I am not just describing individual problems or psychopathology that may occur for working class students. I am describing a pathology in American social and educational systems that *shows up* in people who go against the grain that can punish people in college from working class backgrounds.
>
> (p. 166)

Jensen (2012) talks about "resisting" as one of the coping strategies people use in an attempt to resolve the conflict between old and new worlds. "Resistance to the dominant middle class culture is harder to track than distancing because it often manifests in the act of *not* going to college, *not* writing papers, and so on" (p. 169). I have also come to see the act of not writing as my own silent act of working-class resistance, of not buying into the full middle-class value system. Not advancing in status and salary may have also relieved some survivor guilt, another potential risk of crossing class identified by Jensen (2012). If I feel "underpaid" within the academic world, I may feel less of a traitor to my working-class roots. I am not reaping the full benefits of my class crossing, thus mediating my survivor guilt around "making it." These unconscious methods of navigating my old and new worlds have not served me. My struggle around publishing and advancing in rank has been long standing and difficult, amplifying my sense of shame and failure over time.

If I Belong Here, Can I Still Be All of Who I Am?

The CLCI Writing Group has helped me to break through an invisible but powerful barrier that I have railed against for years. In the CLCI Writing Group, I had a place of belonging that I longed for but had not found in my academic world. Jensen (2012) identifies one of the issues for class crossovers as anomie: a sense of placelessness, a sense of not being at home anywhere. My sense of "not belonging" in the academic environment has been ever present, despite the fact that my teaching evaluations by students and response by peers observing my teaching indicate that I am a skilled professor in the classroom and in advising.

The lonely act of writing for publication was beset by fears of inadequacy, which were transformed for me as I participated in the CLCI Writing Group. The very nature of the CLCI program allowed us to be present as human beings in the room, people doing the difficult work of learning about ourselves in order to make room for all of our students in the curriculum and teaching process.

The CLCI Writing Group gave me a place of belonging, where I could be authentically present and genuinely explore and discover both about my teaching and myself. It was important and helpful for me that one of the leaders also came from a working-class background. This shared experience—and trusting that my experience would be understood, valued and accepted—forged my affiliation with and commitment to the group. At one point, a deadline was set by which everyone needed to have a first draft completed. I had many small pieces written, but nothing near a first draft. If I could not make this deadline, I would not be able to continue in the group process, and my group membership was a very motivating factor. It was both the presence of the group that allowed me to discover what I needed to write as well as the presence of the group that helped me find a place of belonging from which I could value what I had to write. Having people that I respected accompany me in my process—urging me on, letting me know that they were excited about what I was exploring and writing—helped to counterbalance the internal doubt and shame that had prevented me from continuing on in past attempts.

Through this process, I have been able to come to a richer understanding of the personal conflict I have been caught in. I can now make choices more freely that honor and own my working-class values as well as allow me to navigate the world of academia with more awareness and success. I feel freed to make use of both my working-class skills as well as the advantages that are available to me in an academic position. I do not have to resist publishing in order to stay true to my family, but I can use my new place of privilege to honor, value, and teach about important working-class values.

Conclusion

> They have found ways to resist class amnesia, and to use their working-class identity and consciousness as tools to shape culture.
>
> —Zandy (1995, p. 1)

Working through my own class amnesia and bringing the gifts of my working-class roots to consciousness has profoundly strengthened my teaching, especially my teaching about social class. Most recently, I developed a new class assignment that seems to engage both an intellectual analysis and provide a vehicle for experiencing aspects of the affective, lived experience of class stratification. I divided my students into small working groups, gave them a Monopoly game, and asked them to rewrite the rules of the game to make it more "true to life." For example, we do not all begin in life having the same amount of money as players do in Monopoly. The next step was for the students to play the game incorporating these more "true to life" rules. The process of changing the rules engaged the students in thinking about and discussing our social structures and differences in the lived experience of social classes. The process of playing the game brings to the surface some of the underlying feelings of class differences. One participant, who had very limited resources in the Monopoly game, reported that she felt very distant and uninvolved from the other players. She could not participate in buying property given her low financial resources, and she reported feeling that she was playing a completely different game from the rest of her group. We discussed how true to life that must feel for many in our consumerist culture.

In real life, social classes are frequently divided, living in separate neighborhoods and attending different schools. In Monopoly, the participants are able to see the reality of all players as they move around the board, their financial struggles or abundance. Nothing is hidden. The visibility of the struggles frequently, though not always, stirred the desire to help their fellow players. Students would create social service programs to support those with limited resources, for example, they would get special funds when passing Go. Not ironically, students often noted that the "safest" place on the board for those with very low income was in jail, as they did not risk any increasing costs while on that space. One person who was very destitute reported his choices as either "waiting for a hand out" or stealing, and he chose to steal money from another player. Seeing the realities of each player's options as they travel around the board brought a greater awareness of the impact of financial difference on lived experiences.

Unlike my earlier attempts to teach about social class, which either engaged people affectively but without a solid intellectual understanding or remained only in the intellectual/cognitive realm without any personal or affective engagement, this Monopoly exercise created an experience that integrated the intellectual and affective experiences of social class. My own "integration" of an understanding of the class tensions I was straddling within myself has led to a more integrated, rich learning experience for my students.

Questions for Reflection

1. How do you name your class background? What are the strengths and the challenges of that identity?
2. What is the range of class backgrounds in your classrooms? In what ways do these social and economic identities impact your teaching methods?
3. How has class identity informed your approach to research? Writing? Professional practice?

References

hooks, b. (2000). *Where we stand: Class matters*. New York, NY: Routledge.
Jensen, B. (2012). *Reading classes: On culture and classism in America*. Ithaca, NY: Cornell University Press.
Pappano, L. (2015, April 8). First-generation students unite. *The New York Times*, p. ED18.
Zandy, J. (Ed.). (1995). *Liberating memory: Our work and our working-class consciousness*. New Brunswick, NJ: Rutgers University Press.

Section II

Pedagogy and the Other

5   Learning as the *Other*

A Lesson in Human Fragility

Meenakshi Chhabra

I want to know, as fully and exactly as I can, what the wound is and how much [we are] suffering from it.

—W. Berry (1989)

My Introduction to Race in the United States

When I moved from India to the U.S. in the early '90s, I was intrigued by how people were often talked about as white, brown, black, yellow, and red. It reminded me of the steel spice box in my mother's kitchen in India. The round box had six small containers, each for a different color spice: red chili, yellow turmeric, light brown coriander, dark brown cumin, and the black mustard seeds, all neatly packed around the white salt container, which was always in the center. The initial fascination with the color description soon faded away, as I slowly acculturated into a racialized society. Sometimes by speaking and sometimes by being silent, I learned to navigate my way as the racial *other*, through a complex terrain of race.

Almost a decade later, I was hired as a faculty at Lesley University. I teach graduate courses focusing on identity, culture, and the politics of differences in relation to immigration, race, gender, class, and sexual orientation in the United States and issues of conflict transformation in a global context. Perhaps because of my own experiences with difference and because I see myself as a scholar-practitioner, I am conscious and deliberate about bringing a lens of self-reflection and social justice to my classroom. I strongly hold these as the purpose of higher education. On one hand, as an immigrant and an outsider, I have a sense of ease in engaging in these conversations; on the other, as a faculty of Color in a predominantly white institution (PWI), this has not been a smooth journey. As a new faculty, concern for my teaching evaluations and of being perceived as anti-White have challenged me in finding effective ways of engaging in conversations about difference. In the beginning, I dealt with this by taking a purely academic stance to the discussions, staying in the safe space of the head, and trying to manage my own emotions. With time, experience, and participating in the Cultural Literacy Curriculum Institute (CLCI), I gained the comfort, skills, and collegial support to integrate the readings with deeper and courageous discussions on difference, while being fully aware of my vulnerabilities. Over the years, the syllabi and pedagogy have gone through several iterations. In this essay, I am presenting snapshots from the process, a work still in progress.

Setting the Space—CLCI and Cultural Humility

Some of the principles of CLCI I have embraced in my classroom practices are building trust and a sense of community, starting with an inquiry of the self, and encouraging reflection on the interdependence between self and other and its interplay with the larger sociopolitical context. These principles are firmly grounded in the concept of cultural humility, which asks the question, "how can I better understand the other through this experience?" Cultural humility is defined as "an ability to maintain an interpersonal stance that is other-oriented (or open to the other) in relation to aspects of cultural identity that are most important to the [person]" (Hook, Davis, Owen, Worthington, & Utsey, 2013, p. 2).

The concept may seem naïve about power differences in social interactions. Cultural humility originated in the healthcare field and has been adapted especially for nurses, therapists, and social workers to enhance the quality of their interactions with their clients and community members. The three main elements of cultural humility clarify where the ownership and responsibility lies: a lifelong commitment to self-evaluation and self-critique, fix power imbalances, and develop partnerships with people and groups who advocate for others (Waters & Asbill, 2013). In light of these principles, I have expanded the definition as "An ability to maintain an interpersonal stance that is other-oriented (or open to the other) in relation to aspects of cultural identity that are most important to the [person]," *especially those aspects that trigger in us a sense of unearned privilege about ourselves and an implicit prejudice about the other.* This is how I apply the concept in my graduate classroom.

The CLCI has also validated for me the use of opening and closings, experiential activities, creative expression, and participatory pedagogy. I weave these into the weekly class sessions. Each class is bookended with a structured opening and a closing to create a sense of stepping in and out of our shared learning space. These openings and closings include a few minutes of silence, a song, or reading of a poem or a quote. In the first few sessions,

I spend some time each week on community building. Students collectively frame five to six core guidelines for classroom discussions, which are posted in the classroom every week. Some other examples of such activities are asking them to narrate the story of their name using the poem *Where I'm From* (Lyon, 1993) as a prompt to write about their backgrounds, talking about their school and neighborhood experience, or sharing about someone who has deeply influenced their life. While these activities might sound trivial and time consuming for a graduate classroom, I have witnessed their value in creating a safe classroom space for authentic conversations. These activities also complement the course content in deepening students' understanding of the relationship between self and other, which I believe is crucial in effectively responding to issues of difference.

Confronting My Implicit Bias in a Different Context

My own experience of uncovering bias and privilege has helped me wrestle with the dynamic of self and other and contributed to my teaching in a significant way. One of these unforgettable experiences took place a few years ago when I was in India on a research project. The project was in the Old City of Delhi in a predominantly Muslim neighborhood, a place I did not know well. I was collecting data and conducting workshops in schools in the area. Most of the children in these schools are Muslims and belong to families that are struggling financially. Due to structural concerns, one of the elementary schools I was working in had been temporarily relocated to a different neighborhood, which was predominantly Hindu. Besides being very crowded, the new location also had a reputation of being a drug-dealing hub. This made the teachers very concerned about the safety of their students who walked to school, sometimes three miles one way.

On this particular day, a young boy around nine years old came to the staff room and presented his application to the vice-principal requesting an early dismissal. I overheard the conversation as the vice-principal reminded him to be safe when he walked home, to which the young boy confidently replied, "Madam please don't worry. I will go from the Muslim quarters. I know that route. My mother showed it to me. I know how to avoid the Hindu area." I was pained as I listened to his words, but not surprised. At this young age, he had learned what he needed to know to be safe as a Muslim minority in India. It saddened me to see a young child needing to think about his safety as a daily routine, and it was difficult to accept that I had a role in it.

I would have probably not had the same response had I witnessed the situation three decades ago. I thought I understood the politics of difference as an undergraduate student in India, coming from a struggling working-class family, having heated intellectual debates on political issues over cups of tea in the college cafeteria with people who thought like me. I was raised a Hindu (the dominant religion in India) and grew up in predominantly Hindu neighborhoods. Even when we lived in Muslim-dominated communities, there were clear lines dividing the lived spaces, and interactions across those divides were measured (Gupta, 2008). The perceptions about Muslims in India are further complicated because they share the religious identity with people from Pakistan, a country which has the status of enemy nation for Indians. Muslims in India as such are seen as the enemy, and stereotypes about them as not to be trusted remain largely unchallenged in the social discourse (Kumar, 2001).

If I had witnessed the young boy's response during my undergraduate years, perhaps I would have denied and dismissed his experience. I might have said, "This is what they teach them at home. This is why they cannot integrate. India is a secular country; then how can these children think like that? Why do they have to feel unsafe, they will never change," and so on. My being the other in the United States had given me a window into the experience of the other in a different context. I bring these experiences into my teaching and pedagogy with a hope to encourage my students to recognize their own hidden biases.

Race Talk in My Classroom

While race and racism in the United States is a full course in our program I also spend two to three sessions on the topic in the middle of my course. Since I began teaching the course, there has been an increase in the ethnic and racial diversity in the class. However, I seldom have Black students and feel the void of that experience in discussions on race in the United States. Most of the students continue to be predominantly White. While different students share their perspectives on the topic of race based on their racial identity and their particular contexts, for scope and purpose of this essay, I am focusing on the White students' experiences in class.

Although many of my White students have been living in a "diverse" society, for the majority of them, my course is the first time they confront issues of race and racism in a structured setting. Several researchers, both Black and White, have talked about this phenomenon, calling it a self-protective silence of "racial privilege," a "White insulation," and such. In addressing this issue, I have found it helpful to ground the teaching of this module in two theoretical concepts: the concept of *Dignity* as explained by Hicks (2011), and *White Privilege*. Recent research affirms that teaching about White Privilege in a PWI can be transformative for White students (Boatright-Horowitz, Frazier, Harps-Logan, & Crockett, 2013). Although the course might seem one-sided, I believe my students get a plethora of dominant messages from the world that surrounds them, and I see it as my academic commitment to introduce them to counter narratives with which they are unfamiliar. I have often wondered how my White colleagues would orient the course.

Before I begin the sessions, I ask students to share in small groups what they know about race in general, about race and racism in the United States, and the burning questions they have on the topic. This helps me understand my students' starting points and assumptions so I can thread these into discussions that follow. Here I will share some of the activities, prompts, and resources I use for this module.

Dignity Model

Drawing on the Dignity model by Hicks, which the students have been familiarized with, I ask them to share in small groups about a time when they either experienced or witnessed a violation and/or affirmation of dignity. While focus in small groups is on the individual experiences, in large groups I direct questions to help identify patterns and behaviors of what dignity violations and affirmations look like, and the impact these have on people at the receiving end. This provides an overarching frame and gives a language for the activities and conversations.

The Bus Trip

I sometimes require students to travel in groups of three or four on a bus ride from Harvard Square to the inner city of Boston. Although there has been a marked change in the city since I traveled this journey myself as a part of a graduate course on racism, my students' experiences are worth noting and I believe helpful in uncovering their assumptions about racism and the other. For many of the White students, it is their first time venturing into the inner city. I provide them guidelines for the observation, which includes observing people, place, and self. They are required to observe passengers who get on and off the bus and talk to two or three people to learn about the neighborhood. They make a note of the buildings, architecture, schools, restaurants, banks, parks, and empty lots. Lastly, I remind them to be aware of their thoughts and feelings throughout the journey. Students use writing, drawing, photography, and other creative ways to document their experience.

In their reflections, among other things, students talk about noticing the change of color in the bus from predominantly White to people of Color boarding the bus as it approaches the final destination, the changes in the physical space, and the sense of fear they feel when they disembark at the last stop, especially when they walk around in the community. While acknowledging their experiences, I pose questions about their learning from the journey and about what informs their fears. These discussions are particularly revealing to students about connections between race(ism), space, and socialization in White families, communities, and schools, being constantly surrounded by negative stereotypes about Blacks. As a follow up, I will often invite the students to reflect on the experience of school students who are bussed everyday from the inner cities to predominantly White schools in the suburbs, and of people of Color who work everyday in White work places. The conversations usually lead to a discussion on systemic racism. I believe that while it is important for White students to recognize racism as a systemic phenomenon, it is crucial that they are able to reflect on their implicit role in perpetuating it. They also need to think about actions to challenge racism on an individual level.

Jane Eliot, Peggy McIntosh, and Race Implicit Association Test (IAT)[1]

To invite conversations on connections between systemic and individual racism, I complement this module with the film *The Class Divided* (Peters, 1985) based on Jane Eliot's *Blue Eyes Brown Eyes* experiment[2] and Peggy McIntosh's well-known article, *Unpacking White Privilege: Unpacking the Invisible Knapsack* (1988) or the Implicit Association Test (IAT). As a home assignment, students watch a clip on the experiment and rate McIntosh's list of White Privileges in relation to their own experience or complete the Race IAT. When Black students and students of Color are present in class and are willing to share their personal stories of being discriminated against, the discussions across racial divides can provide opportunities for a deep learning for all. I recall one such powerful exchange, which I often use as a case study in this module.

During one of the classes, a Black student shared that during her recent move to a White neighborhood, the neighbors called the police thinking she was an intruder in her new home. A White student, seemingly denying the Black student's experience responded, "That's unbelievable. Can't believe anyone would do that." I remember feeling stunned at that moment and asking myself, "Did this really happen?" I wanted the students to understand the experiences of the other and here they were, out-rightly ignoring it. It was easier for the White students to talk about racism out there than the racism here and now. I also wondered if my perception about the event was guided by my view of that dynamic as a person of Color. Perhaps the White student, by stating that it was "unbelievable," was acknowledging the absurdity of what happened to the Black student. In any case, it was a learning experience and teaching moment that I did not want to lose.

As the conversations continued, I began to think about where I was going to go next. Should I let things be and just go with the flow? Am I being over sensitive because of my own experience as a person of Color in the United

States? What if things get charged and I am not able to handle it? Would I cause more harm? How would the White students, who were the majority in class, perceive me? Fully aware that the conversations will be challenging, and aware of my own vulnerability, I decided to take the risk. After a break and taking permission from the Black student to use what she had shared, I resumed the class by posing questions about what happened, how we responded to what Denise[3] [the Black student] shared, and why it was hard to believe her. The students were not expecting this. After a long pause, one of the White students responded, stating that it felt harsh that someone they knew had to go through something so dehumanizing. Students also voiced concerns about their lack of skills in talking about issues of race, and the absence of private and public structured spaces where both Blacks and Whites could come together to have conversations on the topic. Many of the White students shared that being perceived and called a racist was one of the biggest fears that stopped them from engaging in conversations about race.

Over the years I have also included Di Angelo's *White Fragility* (2011), excerpts from Sue's *Microaggressions in Everyday Life* and *Race Talk* (2010, 2013), and *Racial Microaggressions* by Huber and Solorzano (2015) as required readings for the class. Di Angelo (2011, p. 54) defines White Fragility as,

> a state in which even a minimum amount of racial stress becomes intolerable, triggering a range of defensive moves. These moves include the outward display of emotions such as anger, fear, and guilt, and behaviors such as argumentation, silence, and/or leaving the stress-inducing situation.

She further warns that, "these behaviors, in turn, function to reinstate white racial equilibrium" (2011, p. 54). Making explicit connections between the students' responses and the readings has been very helpful in moving them from being stuck in denial, discomfort, and guilt to acknowledging the everyday racism in their lives.

In the conversations that unfold, students have shared about times they have inadvertently acted in racist ways. Examples include having all White friends in school and being okay with it, being a part of a sorority in college which had all White members, having mostly White friends on Facebook, and refusing a Black colleague's offer to escort them home at night after work because of his race. While these exchanges are often emotional, their honesty and authenticity is also powerful. I have learned to hold the space and, as they say, stay in the fire. I would like to continue the conversations, but the class schedule and syllabus brings us to a close. I know I have just scratched the surface, but I feel confident that the students will now be less hesitant to continue the exchange. We end the class by creating a collective poem with a promise of actions each of us can take in fighting racism in ourselves and in our respective contexts.

White Fragility—Human Fragility

Several researchers have talked about what prevents us from reflecting and taking responsibility of our complicity in systems of oppression. According to Di Angelo, these behaviors are rooted in a binary thinking. Since we equate worthy humans to be all and only good, when we are called out as being racist, it can give rise to an existential fear of feeling amoral and unworthy. The same is also true in the way we equate feeling safe as not feeling uncomfortable. Confronting racism can feel uncomfortable and unsafe. To preserve our perceived sense of worth and safety, we resort to denying our prejudices, justifying our behaviors, and blaming the system for our misconceptions. I call this dynamic *human fragility*. It can apply to any situation when we are made aware of an aspect of our implicit prejudice. We want to see ourselves as worthy humans. The way we preserve this sense of worthiness is by avoiding facing that there are members of groups who are oppressed, and by virtue of our membership in other groups, even as well intentioned people, we play a role in perpetuating the oppression. Hence, we can convince ourselves that we are living a fair, just, and worthy life.

It was this *human fragility*, the fear of losing my sense of worth and comfort, that had come in the way of my confronting my assumptions about Muslims, and also prevented the White student from acknowledging the Black student's experience. The fear of losing what we perceive as our humanity stops us from facing areas in our lives that we feel fragile about, areas where, on account of some aspect of identity, we claim implicit power over others. The paradox is actually true; by looking at our fragilities in the face, we can claim the full human experience and reinforce our humanity.

Next Steps

As I complete this essay, despite the concern of race matters in the United States, I am encouraged to see Black Lives Matter becoming part of the accepted public discourse. University campuses across the country have been forced to bring these discussions to the center stage. It heartens me to see many of my White students and students of Color in these platforms, not sitting on the sideline, but passionately engaging as allies with the Black students and grappling with the insidious nature of biases that encroach the quality of life for so many people.

While individual acts of action and reflection are important, I don't mean to suggest these are enough. Many of the higher education institutions in the United States are still predominantly White. It is pivotal for these institutions, if they seek to respond constructively to issues of difference, to not only focus on increasing the hiring, enrollment, and retention of diverse students, faculty, and staff, but to ask what kind of institutional models and spaces are they fostering within their institutions to support White students, faculty, staff, and administrators to dislodge their implicit racial prejudices.

Questions for Reflection

1. How have you as an educator confronted your own implicit prejudices? How have you encouraged your students to do the same?
2. What suggestions do you have for your institution to effectively respond to challenging issues of difference?

Notes

1 The Race IAT is one of the many tests by Project Implicit developed by Mahazarin Banaji and Tony Greenwald to uncover and educate the public about hidden biases.
2 In 1968 after the assassination of Martin Luther King Jr., Jane Elliot, a third-grade teacher in Iowa decides to teach her students about prejudice. She divided her class into blue-eyed and brown-eyed students privileging one over the other. The experiment had a powerful impact on her students' understanding about race. Since then she has conducted the same experiment with adults in the U.S. and different countries where racial behaviors and attitudes have continued to oppress people of color.
3 Pseudonym.

References

Berry, W. (1989). *The hidden wound*. San Francisco, CA: North Point Press.
Boatright-Horowitz, S. L., Frazier, S., Harps-Logan, Y., & Crockett, N. (2013). Difficult times for college students of color: Teaching white students about white provides hope for change. *Teaching in Higher Education*, *18*(7), 698–708.
DiAngelo, R. (2011). White fragility. *International Journal of Critical Pedagogy*, *3*(3), 54–70.
Gupta, L. (2008, February 8). Growing up Hindu and Muslim: How early does it happen. *Economic and Political Weekly* (online). Retrieved from http://www.epw.in/journal/2008/06/perspectives/growing-hindu-and-muslim-how-early-does-it-happen.html
Hicks, D. (2011). *Dignity: Its essential role in resolving conflict*. New Haven, CT: Yale University Press.

Hook, J. N., Davis, D. E., Owen, J., Worthington, Jr., E. L., & Utsey, S. O. (2013). Cultural humility: Measuring openness to culturally diverse clients. *Journal of Counseling Psychology, 60*(3), 353–366. doi:10.1037/a0032595

Huber, L. P., & Solorzano, D. G. (2015). Racial microaggressions as a tool for critical race research. *Race Ethnicity and Education, 18*(3), 297–320.

Kumar, K. (2001). *Prejudice and pride.* New Delhi: Penguin Books.

Lyon, G. E. (1993). *Where I'm from.* Retrieved from http://www.georgeellalyon.com/where.html

McIntosh, P. (1988). White privilege and male privilege: A personal account of coming to see correspondence through work in women's studies. In M. Anderson & P. Hill Collins (Eds.), *Race, class, and gender: An anthology* (pp. 94–105). Belmont, CA: Wadsworth.

Peters, W. (Producer and Director). (First broadcast March, 1985). *A class divided.* U.S.A. FRONTLINE, WGBH Educational Foundation.

Sue, D. W. (2010). *Microaggressions in everyday life: Race, gender, and sexual orientation.* Hoboken, NJ: John Wiley & Sons.

Sue, D. W. (2013). Race talk: The psychology of racial dialogues. *American Psychologist, 68*(8), 663.

Waters, A., & Asbill, L. (2013, August). Reflections on cultural humility. *American Psychological Association CYF News.* Retrieved from http://www.apa.org/pi/families/resources/ newsletter/2013/08/cultural-humility.aspx

6 Becoming an Ally to Indigenous People

Coleen O'Connell

> *The growing interest in Indigenous knowledge is perhaps directly related to growing concerns about degradation of the environment.*
>
> —June George (2012)

Indigenous Experience

Fred Pollock (name changed for privacy), Passamaquoddy elder and healer, lives in a small house perched on a granite hill overlooking Passamaquoddy Bay at the lower end of Fundy Bay where Canada's Maritime provinces meet the United States. Fred is a member of the Passamaquoddy tribe who has for thousands of years made their home in this boreal forest/marine environment long before there were such countries or the state of Maine. Passamaquoddy literally means "people who spear Pollock." The Passamaquoddy share this region with four other tribes—the Penobscot, Maliseet, Micmac, and Abenaki, who together over the centuries formed the Wabanaki Confederacy—the people of the dawn. Living in the eastern reaches of North America, or Turtle Island, the Wabanaki people have taken the responsibility to raise the sun each morning for all the people and relations of Turtle Island. Living both on the Atlantic coastline and inland in the forests and lakes of the region, the people have navigated the waters, survived, and thrived on the marine life and forest offerings. The land has provided a wealth of plants from which medicine has been extracted over the centuries. Fred Pollock is a collector of medicinal plants in accordance with the teachings of his grandmother. In her final years, she in essence, downloaded orally to her grandson, her knowledge of the plants, when and how to collect them, and how to make the medicines. She chose him as the recipient of her knowledge. Fred has embraced this transmission and in his elder years has become a medicine healer.

Fred has an honorary doctorate degree from a Maine college. He smiles broadly as I greet him with a hug and call him Dr. Pollock when he arrives at the field station for his teaching stint with Lesley University graduate students in the Ecological Teaching and Learning MS program. His smile is disarming, putting all immediately at ease. We help him unload his belongings and then gather for an introduction. He listens generously as students introduce themselves, and he makes comments and sometimes jokes about the information that is shared. People laugh, share stories, and the formalities are dropped. Fred has officially joined our learning community. For the next three days, we will talk with him over meals, go hiking in the woods to gather medicinal plants, will get sticky with the sap of a balsam tree, will climb ladders to tap pine trees, and will sit with him at a Passamaquoddy sacred site as he speaks about his life growing up on the edge of this continent.

Some of his stories are painful to hear. Taken away to a Canadian residential school set up specifically to assimilate Indigenous children, Fred speaks of sexual assault, homicides, beatings, and solitary confinement. For many of the graduate students, this is their first introduction to the violations of Indigenous people at the hands of their colonizers. Tears come to eyes, shock ripples through the group, and guilt finds a bed in the hearts and minds of many. Fred is not afraid to be honest, but he is not intending to lay blame. He is merely sharing his story. Fred has many stories, and in the days that unfold, they are shared either in small groups while hiking through the woods, while eating together at the dining hall, or in the larger group as we sit in a circle. By the time he leaves, most of these teachers can now say they have their first Native American friend. And by sharing so authentically with Fred, the guilt has subsided as they determine that their teaching about Native Americans will never be the same again.

The essential learning for the students in this place-based model of education is that the Passamaquoddy are the first known and documented inhabitants of this place, and they continue to live and thrive in their homeland. Though one of two Passamaquoddy reservations has been reduced to 400 acres along the ocean in a place called Sipyak (Pleasant Point, Maine) their history is recorded across the entire region. Another Passamaquoddy reservation is miles inland in the lakes/woods region. The Passamaquoddy continue to be active participants in the local happenings while they struggle to hold onto their language, their sovereignty, and their identity. As is true with most Indigenous tribes, they are not longing to be assimilated into the dominant western global culture. They want to remain intact within their own culture. However, colonization has placed a heavy toll on them, and assimilation in large degree has been the result. The Passamaquoddy people live in pride in spite of the oppressions they have been dealt and continue to be dealt. I could not possibly bring students to this ecological field program in Maine without introducing them to, and including, the voices of living Indigenous inhabitants. To omit these experiences from the curriculum would be to mis-appropriate understanding of the ecosystem that they have come to study. It is through an experience with Indigenous people that students can begin to identify that their own concerns for the natural world are congruent with the teachings of Native cultures. They begin to see that becoming allies with Native cultures is an act of reciprocity that holds within it a kernel of hope for our world.

In my first days of the field program, I survey my mostly white graduate students. I ask the following questions:

1. How well do you know Native American history in the U.S.? How did you learn what you know?
2. Are you familiar with the Doctrine of Discovery and Manifest Destiny—both concepts within U.S. doctrinal history that have vast influence on the oppression of Indigenous people on this continent?
3. Do you know who are/were the original Native people of where you live?
4. Do you have a Native American friend? What tribe? How did you come to know this person/family?
5. Have you ever visited a Native American reservation or community? Which one(s)? What was your experience?
6. Do you include Indigenous cultures in your teaching curriculum? If so, describe how you do that.

It has been my experience in conducting this survey that most white educators have a very limited understanding or knowledge of Native American history and as a result do not incorporate any Indigenous cultural work into their curriculums. More shocking to me over the years is how many students state that they had no idea that there were still tribes organized and living in America. Most cannot name the local tribe that inhabited the place they now call their home.

Personal Experience

I come to this sensitivity of Native American history from my own family story. My mother's father was a "half-breed"—half Indian and half white. My Indian great grandmother was adopted into a white family at birth, so she had no cultural identification with her Native heritage. She would marry a white man and have eight children. Growing up, my mother was very proud of her Native American ties, though she knew almost nothing about it other than she carried Native features in her face and skin. My father's family often mocked her and called her a "squaw"—a derogatory name for an Indian woman. As a child, I witnessed these moments and realized the shame my mother felt when this happened. But she was undaunted, and she continued to speak always with pride about her Native blood. I loved when we gathered with her uncles, the half-breed brothers of her father, who had died when she was ten years old. The uncles all looked like Native American men, and I cherish the one picture I have of them from a family reunion back in 1958.

They lived assimilated lives and did not in any way identify with anything Native American. It would not be until I was an adult that I would begin to question this story and to explore for myself what had happened in my family. I began to explore my own identity as an earth-loving woman, and my attention to Native American cultures would increase as I began to feel my tribal roots within my own identity and ancestry. I began to seek out Native American people in my home region in order to explore the misconceptions I had been taught within my public school education. Though I do not identify as Native American, I have felt a deep calling to right a wrong in the way we educate about Indigenous people in our education programs.

Becoming an environmental educator has afforded me the platform in which to correct the ways in which we teach about Indigenous people. As I came to understand the degradation of the environments of planet Earth, I began to also understand that Indigenous cultures had a well-developed ethic brought from thousands of years living and thriving with the land. Indigenous knowledge and rights emerged as a platform in Agenda 21 of the Earth Summit that was held in Rio de Janeiro in 1992, calling on educators around the world to infuse their curriculums with the historical knowledge and understanding of the role of Indigenous people in maintaining our balance with Earth's systems. Agenda 21 is a nonbinding, voluntarily implemented action plan of the United Nations with regard to sustainable development. It is an action agenda for the UN, other multilateral organizations, and individual governments around the world that can be executed at local, national, and global levels. The "21" in Agenda 21 refers to the twenty-first century. It has been affirmed and modified at subsequent UN conferences (Wikipedia, 2016).

Student Experience

While this was a global groundbreaking moment for Indigenous people around the world, my graduate program at Lesley University in Environmental Education had for years already been practicing cultural humility and sensitivity as we traveled around the country in a school bus studying the ecosystems of North America. It was imperative as we arrived in each new bioregion of the continent that we make contact with, and learn from, the Indigenous culture that inhabited the region. Whether Navajo and Hopi elders and families in Arizona, Pueblo people in New Mexico, Lakota political leaders in South Dakota, Makah fisherman in Washington State, each bioregion has a rich history of the Native Americans that call that place home. It would be in these intimate encounters in the homes of these Native people that I would come to learn a story about Indigenous people in my country that was not taught to me in my public school education or affirmed in my family of origin.

It would be in those experiences that I would begin to both be angered by the injustices but empowered to become an ally to Native people in how I educated any audience I taught thereafter. I was inspired then to create a program for educators that would tell a new story about the places they lived and taught. I would insert Native history, but more importantly, Native voices into the experience to become part of the curriculum in a different way than teepees at Thanksgiving and Pocahontas as a Native super heroine. Not only would I encourage teachers to become friends with Native people, but to go further and become allies. In becoming an ally, we use our own white privilege to speak out about injustices, to teach culturally accurate history, and create a consciousness about the rightful place of Indigenous people in our diverse country.

Within the integrated model of the program I have been directing for eighteen years, the Ecological Teaching and Learning MS program, the pedagogical framework is one of a transdisciplinary nature. Ecology lends itself as a science that has ties to all other disciplines. As the program sets out to enhance ecological literacy in its graduate students, it assumes that such knowledge will have ripple effects out to the audiences that are taught by these individuals. We begin the program with a three-week intensive to get to know a place—usually a place that is unfamiliar to the students. In this way, they have a level of cognitive dissonance that allows them to see the place with fresh eyes. In a carefully orchestrated schedule, students are exposed to the geology, climate, and natural history of the place. They write and sketch learning about a place from the various perspectives that are not limited to the scientific. Added to this is the introduction and engagement with the people who inhabit this place, which is the context for the time spent with Fred Pollock.

Eighteen years into the facilitation of this graduate experience, I have become, first and foremost, friends with many Native peoples, Fred being just one. In the enduring length of my relationship with him, I model for my students an important aspect of breaking down the barriers of culture. I model a reciprocal and enduring relationship with someone that is "other." I bring to consciousness the idea that Native people are alive and well in our home places and that we can become friends. That we can share in our understanding of place—each giving to the other what it is we have to offer. We can then become allies in ways that were unknown to us before making an intention to be inclusive of Indigenous history and knowledge.

When the students return to their home places from the field program, one of their fall assignments is to discover who the Indigenous people are in their bioregion. It is in this assignment that I begin to explore with students how to become an ally to Native people. It starts with research and curiosity. Where do they begin to piece together this story? Google, historical records at the town library, books written by local authors, and organizations in the area all contribute to this knowledge. They are also encouraged to begin to read Native authors. They might not be authors from their bioregion, but Native writers are numerous and their books cross a wide spectrum of knowledge that is valuable to the curious educator. Some authors are not Native, but what they offer to our cultural literacy education is critical. I have a book list that gives my own personal favorites that has been essential reading for me on my journey to become an ally to Native people: *A People's History of the US* by Howard Zinn; *Crazy Brave* by Joy Harjo; *Custer Died for Your Sins* and *God Is Red* by Vine Deloria, Jr.; *Black Elk Speaks* by John Niehardt; *Bury My Heart at Wounded Knee* by Dee Brown; *Look to the Mountain* and *Native Science* by Gregory Cajete; *All Our Relations* by Winona LaDuke; all novels by Louise Erdrich; *Thinking in Indian: A John Mohawk Reader* by John Mohawk; Passamaquoddy history books by Donald Soctomah; and my new favorite, *Braiding Sweetgrass* by Robin Wall Kimmerer. I tell students that if they google Native American authors, they will find a long list of writers and their tribal identity. The internet can offer students an incredible education just by searching. And in reading the books, you begin to understand the Doctrine of Discovery, Manifest Destiny, Native sovereignty, treaty violations, tribal differences, but more importantly, the common theme that runs through all the literature: the interconnected and sacred relationship that Native people hold with all of creation. It is in this realization that ecologically focused students begin to see their own identities and personal visions tied to those of Native people. It is in these moments of awareness that becoming an ally to Native people becomes imperative. We are all One.

I am often asked by students—how do I meet and befriend a Native person? How did I come to know Fred? Or my other Native friends? My answer is complicated, but it begins by setting the intention of doing just that. By beginning to pay attention to the history and presence of Native people in their bioregion, educators can begin to search for Native organizations or Native presentations that are offered locally. I tell them to find social events where Native people are present and as speakers, workshop leaders, Pow Wows, protests, or any event sponsored by the local tribe. By supporting Native craftspeople, artists, and attending events, there are multiple ways to come to support and know Native people. Native tribes often have museums and visitor centers. Again, the internet becomes a valuable tool in discovering the depth of the topic.

One Student's Reflection

The success of such teaching is illustrated with this journal entry from Cristina LaRue's reflective practice coursework:

> Though I have lived on the island for over five years and attended many community and cultural events I had never attended the annual Pow Wow at Aquinnah. I had always been interested in going but felt awkward—that I would be out of place, not welcome, or looked at as a white woman viewing Wampanoag culture as a spectacle, unable to participate authentically. I worried I would be unintentionally co-opting Wampanoag culture. And so each year I convinced myself the "open public invitation" was simply a courtesy and my attendance would not be appropriate.
>
> After my time in Maine this past summer I had a different perspective and comfort in reaching out and getting to know our local Wampanoag community. One of our Indigenous speakers, during our time in Maine, encouraged us to connect with our local Native people and become allies. A Native couple had welcomed us, total strangers, into their home at Indian Township and shared a pipe ceremony. Fred healed us, body and soul, as we harvested yarrow in his yard at Sipyak and listened to his stories at Split Rock. Perhaps more than any other, our experiences with these Native people changed me, healed me, and inspired me to find ways to be an ally to my Wampanoag neighbors here at home. When I read in the calendar section of our local newspaper that the Aquinnah Pow Wow was coming up I decided my first step would be to finally accept the invitation I had turned down year after year.
>
> We parked along the Aquinnah circle, a familiar place atop the famous cliffs, and took in the view of Moshop Beach, the Atlantic, and out to Noman's Land. As we crossed the field to the tents we were welcomed by drumming and singing, a food stand advertising bluefish dinners with squash, corn cakes, and sassafras tea, and a jewelry stand with beautiful wampum necklaces. People were dressed traditionally, adorned with feathers and beautifully beaded dresses. And people were dressed contemporarily with jeans and leather, tattoos and piercings. Children ran and laughed, babies cried, friends and relatives greeted each other joyfully. And when we approached the entrance tent we were greeted with a warm smile that immediately eased my nerves and affirmed that I was in fact welcome.
>
> Over the loud speaker the announcer called out, "Intertribal dancers to the tent" and people of all ages in modern and traditional dress circle danced and chatted as the men drummed and sang. The dance was

nothing impressive on the surface; to the untrained eye it appeared to simply be an energetic stepping on beat with the drums. But the music, the voices, the dress, the steps, the faces, all gave me a sense of the deep tradition and connection through movement to thousands of years of shared history I was witnessing.

After the dances we walked around chatting with friends who shared their surprise that it was our first time at the Pow Wow. As we passed people in Wampanoag Mashpee shirts and overheard conversations about busses and ferries back to the mainland I realized that the Pow Wow drew tribe members from the Cape as well. I wondered how the current casino issue might be impacting the energy at the Pow Wow. Recently the tribe took a vote on whether or not to continue to pursue a casino on MV tribal lands. Island dwelling tribe members voted against it but were outnumbered by tribe members living off-island. Just last week a pile of dead skunks was deposited in front of the Wampanoag Tribe marker at the start of the reservation. Though the climate was joyful I wondered what tensions and stresses might have been temporarily pushed aside in honor of the celebration.

The food stand we chose was run by Wampanoag from off-island. As one person worked, three smoked cigarettes and snacked, despite the long line of patrons. One woman with many piercings and tattoos argued with her co-workers and checked watermarks on $20 bills. She had a beautiful wolf tattoo covering one arm and "Wampanoag" tattooed across her bare shoulders. I found myself climbing my familiar ladder of inference—making judgments and assumptions that confirmed what our culture has taught us—she must do drugs, she must be an alcoholic, she must be lazy and looking for an easy paycheck, she must be the one who votes for a casino on tranquil, sacred lands. I caught myself and immediately was ashamed. I thought of Fred and his story. I thought of the generations of abuse and discrimination tribal members across our country and Canada suffered and its lasting, multigenerational psychological and physical effects. I wondered who her grandparents might be and what challenges they faced. I wondered what it might be like to have your culture, land, ancestors, and relatives, attacked and subdued, manipulated and murdered. And I realized I had no idea what carrying that history could possibly be like. All my assumptions about this stranger had no grounding in who she was, but only in who our culture thinks she should be. Though I am ashamed I was so quick to judge, I am thankful for those who have opened my eyes to help me see more clearly and opened my heart to feel more empathetically. As I listened to the drums behind me I gave thanks for being there, in that moment.

I gave thanks for Fred and other Passamaquoddy people I had met in Maine for sharing their love and their stories with me. I gave thanks for our Lesley Ecological Teaching and Learning cohort for the opportunity to look deeply within, without judgment, and to share this journey. And I gave thanks for my ability to break out of old, harmful thought patterns and take part in a beautiful celebration of the history and tradition of our island home.

If educators are teaching in a classroom, they can start by inviting a Native person to present to their class. I explain that they shouldn't just do it once, but multiple times. Each time, the relationship with the Native person becomes stronger, more familiar, and a friendship begins to form. It starts in the small steps but can be enlarged to a long-standing friendship that can include personal invitations to join in other events. This has been my own personal experience. I have to show up, be present, be open to the comfort level of the Native person, and be authentic and genuine in my desire to be friends. Is this any different than starting a friendship with anyone? It is not different with Native people.

Conclusion

Becoming aware of Native history, different from the one most of us were taught in our American History courses, will hopefully provoke a desire to speak in support of Native initiatives moving us from friendship to being an ally. Supporting the efforts of Native people around the world to retain sovereignty of their lands, to prevent further degradation of Earth, and to honor the diversity that makes our planet operate in healthy systems, is to speak for oneself. There is no separation. Native people ask us to have gratitude for Mother Earth and to arise each day in thanksgiving. Such a simple request. So easy to begin becoming an ally today.

What Native people want for their children, I want for mine. In this way, we can work together to ensure that future generations will have what they need to sustain them. We have only to look to our Native neighbors to find comrades in this uphill battle to save the planet for all life. We are all related.

Questions for Reflection

In conclusion, I ask you, the reader, to reflect on and answer for yourself the survey questions I ask students:

1. How well do you know Native American History in the U.S.? How did you learn what you know?

2. Are you familiar with the Doctrine of Discovery and Manifest Destiny—both concepts within U.S. doctrinal history that have vast influence on the oppression of Indigenous people on this continent?
3. Do you know who are/were the original Native people of where you live?
4. Do you have a Native American friend? What tribe? How did you come to know this person/family?
5. Have you ever visited a Native American reservation or community? Which one(s)? What was your experience?
6. Do you include Indigenous cultures in your teaching curriculum? If so, describe how you do that.

References

George, J. (2012). Indigenous knowledge as a component of the school curriculum. In L. M. Semali & J. Kincheloe (Eds.), *What is Indigenous knowledge: Voices from the academy* (p. 79). New York: Routledge.

Wikipedia. (2016). Agenda 21. Retrieved from http://en.wikipedia.org/wiki/Agenda_21

7   Seizing Teachable Moments

An African American Professor's Reflections of Conversations on Race and Culture With White Students

M. Francine Jennings

Introduction

Over the past twelve years, I have functioned in the capacity of both adjunct faculty and National Faculty at Lesley University, a private university in Cambridge, Massachusetts. This means that I have had the distinct pleasure of teaching courses across the United States for the division of Creative Arts in Learning (CAL) as a part of the Graduate School of Education. As a professor of arts integration, I teach practicing K–12 educators to incorporate a variety of arts disciplines into core curriculum areas. For the most part, my travels take me to southern, midwestern, northeastern, and western states. The ages of my students range from twenty-five to sixty, with an average age of forty-two. Mirroring current public school national teacher demographics, overwhelmingly my students are middle class, white, and female. Undoubtedly, these assignments have been and continue to be nothing less than gratifying, offering opportunities for meeting new people, for venturing into new geographical territories, and for expanding my teaching into new dimensions.

Raised partially in North Carolina, Virginia, and Washington DC, respectively, each area, technically, is considered to be a southern locality. At this writing, I am residing in the Atlanta, Georgia metropolitan area; therefore, undeniably, I describe myself as a "girl raised in the south" or a "GRIT" for short. As a person of color and of African American descent, I have been called colored, Negro, Black American, black, Afro-American and African American; however, although I tend not to intellectually belabor the appropriateness of these labels, my inclination is to refer to myself as black or African American. I am also a self-described heterosexual female reared by a loving extended family alongside soundtracks of segregation, discrimination, bigotry, prejudice, and forced integration; yet, in spite of these condescending realities, I was continually discouraged from hating and was always encouraged to achieve two things: (1) get a good education and (2) treat everyone with respect and honor.

Very often, I find myself working in cities or towns where there are very few, if any, people who look like me, and it is even more common to find myself teaching in classrooms where I am the only person of color in the room. I must admit, as one who travailed during the Civil Rights Movement in the position of both observer and participant, I would be remiss if I did not confront one single audacious realization: I have become accustomed to knowing, feeling, and internalizing the spaces I occupy as the only person of color. In fact, I embrace it as part of my earthly existence; consequently, I have made a conscious decision to use this unique position to my advantage as an instructor. To this end, I have been not only pleasantly surprised, but also consistently gratified in discovering how my presence as an African American professor from the South has presented itself as a segue into creating meaningful teachable moments to frame broader issues pertaining to race, cultural identity, and class. In keeping with this line of thought, I have listed a few comments and questions asked by my students over the past twelve years:

1. Do you feel weird being the only African American person in this city/ class?
2. I love the way you talk . . . it makes you seem so friendly and warm.
3. Why is it okay for black people to call each other the "N" word but we [white people] can't do it?
4. We're glad you're from the south. You understand us better than those professors from the north.
5. We can't move like you because we're just regular white people.
6. Since you're a professor, I'm sure you've never had anyone to discriminate against you.
7. This is the first time we've ever had a black professor . . . you're so knowledgeable. You're really articulate and dress really nice.

There are some who might consider the above-mentioned statements and questions as shocking, startling, or perhaps blatantly insulting, but I have preferred to look at them as opportunities to broaden and magnify the scope of cultural clarity, particularly as they relate to educating children and youth in the twenty-first century. Howard (2006) corroborated my sentiments, commenting, "we have neither gone far enough in our analysis of the issues nor deep enough in our design of possible responses" (p. 5). Howard's statement resonates with me as a confirmation of sorts—a confirmation that there is a place for my brand of "cultural seeking and finding."

That said, I would like to examine the deliberate processes I choose to employ when confronted with student inquiries and questions pertaining to race, class, and culture.

Assessing underlying meanings—The act of assessing underlying meanings helps me to avoid making unnecessary assumptions;

additionally, it opens a passageway for me to remain consciously objective and reflective as I attempt to process likely implications or intentions related to appropriate or perceived inappropriate questions and statements. By releasing unwarranted assumptions, I tend to give myself permission to entertain fresh possibilities rather than bind myself to self-proclaimed probabilities. Festinger's (1957) cognitive dissonance theory suggests that people tend to avoid hearing ideas conflicting with their own; yet, my intense need to usher in all potential ideas comes across as unmistakably antithetical to Festinger's overarching premise. I actually want to hear thoughts contrary to my own! When listening to students, therefore, I gear myself toward assessment of motive and content, which often happens simultaneously. In assessing motive, for example, I construct "thinking probes" such as those that follow: Is the student genuinely serious? Could the student be using this statement or question to elicit a particular response from me? Could this be a rhetorical question? Could the question or statement be intended to gain recognition from classmates? From there, I very quickly move into evaluating the content of the question or comment utilizing similar levels of scrutiny: Are there terms, phrases, or words in the content in need of clarification? Is the content meant to be received literally or figuratively? Does the content hold stereotypical, prejudicial, or discriminatory overtones? Does the content connect to previous discussions?

Humor—Although over a hundred theories of humor have been acknowledged (Schmidt & Williams, 1971), I am inclined to believe that my brand of humor is tied most closely to relief theory (Schaeffer, 1981) and incongruent resolution theory (Boyd, 2004). Relief theory is inextricably bound by the idea that humor, more specifically laughter, tends to relieve nervous feelings in human beings. For certain, I find that stiffness, rigidity, and tension regularly accompany exchanges pertaining to matters of race, culture, and class; therefore, I am purposeful in infusing humor. Undoubtedly, I have detected that my insertion of humor tends to relax the environment and sends my students a signal that we can discuss any given topic without anxiety or tension. On the other hand, Boyd's incongruity resolution theory encompasses a two-pronged meaning: People laugh at situations (1) because of the element of surprise and (2) because they realize that the incongruity can be resolved or interpreted in a different way than expected. I have seen this theory unfold into practice as I "play" with students during conversations embedded with recognizably sober and serious content. I have found that the humor serves to contain somewhat of an unexpected, yet refreshing shift in the topic's tone while maintaining the integrity of content.

Reframing questions and statements for clarity—The process of reframing questions and statements falls directly under the umbrella of active listening, a term drawn, to a great extent, from the counseling tradition. Carl Rogers' (1951) person-centered theory transmits the connotation that a person should first listen to another person and then respond to that person using techniques such as paraphrasing or restating the original content in a different way. Rogers' theory emphasizes that proper application of this strategy is highly evidentiary of empathy and is soundly indicative of uncompromised listening and understanding. As a minority teacher, this approach has proven to be one of the most valuable. For example, when paraphrasing statements, most of my students thank me for taking the time and making the effort to respect their individual thoughts; simultaneously, the mindful acts of rewording, restating, and rephrasing have the propensity to awaken students to monumental possibilities for unforeseeable "aha" moments. In fact, Rogers asserted that paraphrasing propels people to explore their own attitudes and reactions at a higher level than usual. Personally, I see this as a major thread in the shaping, molding, and growing of personal beliefs and individual perceptions.

Probing to discover new information/creating opportunities for participation—The idea of probing for more information is somewhat synonymous with the craft of good teaching. As educators, we are taught to continually assess, examine, question, inquire, and explore. Should these factors not exist, we become mere lecturers or depositors of information (Freire, 1970), diminishing and eliminating foundations for cognitive expansion and creative exchange. I have discovered, similar to active listening, that probing for more information emerges as a compelling strategy for gathering ideas and opinions that may not have otherwise surfaced; more importantly, deliberate probing validates an atmosphere that releases open and honest participation.

In order to elucidate various means by which the above-mentioned processes may materialize, I have offered scripts of two student–teacher exchanges. The first exchange, which I will refer to as Dialogue #1, took place in a small northwestern state right at the end of a fifteen-minute class break.

Dialogue #1

Student 1: Don't you feel weird being the only black person in this class? (*Initial question*)

Teacher: Actually, I feel pretty weird whether I'm the only black person or not! (*Humor*) But all jokes aside, by "weird" are you asking if I feel uncomfortable? (*Assessing underlying meanings*)

Student 1: Sorta! You don't "spazz out" when you don't see other black people? (*Student expands the initial question*)

Teacher: Well, I do like to see other black people, but I'm okay if I don't. (*Conversation begins to evolve; other students begin to attend to the exchange*)

Student 1: I don't know if I could do that! (*Student begins to redirect the initial question to himself*)

Teacher: Do you mean that it would be difficult if you were the only white person in a group of people who were racially different from you? (*Reframing the statement for clarity*)

Student 1: I just couldn't do it. It would freak me out! (*Student provides a direct answer*)

Teacher: Sounds like it would make you very uncomfortable. Do you have any idea why you feel that way? (*Probing for additional information*) I would love to hear feelings from the rest of you as well. (*Creating opportunities for group participation*)

Student 1: I just have always been around people like myself and it feels scary to think I'm in the minority. (*Student transparency*)

Student 2: Yeah, we just aren't used to being around people different from ourselves. (*Student transparency*)

Student 3: But, I lived in Atlanta for a while, so I'm used to seeing all kinds of people. I like it out here but there's no diversity. Everybody looks the same, believes in the same thing, and sees life the same way. I don't like that. (*Student transparency*)

Teacher: I can appreciate that. There are many people who feel exactly like you. Are there others in class who share similar feelings? Different feelings? (*More students begin to share their various backgrounds and experiences*) So, it sounds like some of you have been exposed to more diverse populations than others, and those of you who have had more experiences with diversity appear to have a higher comfort level with being in the minority than those of you who have had fewer experiences. I lived in the south during the period of school desegregation, so I became accustomed to being the only person of color at an early age. I was also exposed to people from diverse nationalities as I traveled with my family and attended college. So, to answer the original question, I guess I don't feel exceptionally weird. It's just my natural way of being. (*Transparency*)

So, what might all this mean if we're teaching students who may be the only person of color, the only person of a particular ethnicity, or maybe the only person from a particular cultural background? (*Aligning the conversation with teaching children*)

Student 1: I guess I shouldn't think they're uncomfortable or feel bad just because they look different. Sometimes, I bend over backwards because I feel sorry for them. (*Student introspection*)

Teacher: Kinda like you were feeling sorry for me? (*Probing for additional information*)

Student 1: Exactly!

Student 2: Yeah, we make so many assumptions about our kids based on how we would feel . . . it's not really fair. (*Student introspection*)

Teacher: So Student 1, look what you started! We now know that just because a student is a minority in your classroom community, he or she may not necessarily feel uncomfortable. We also know that our lived experiences may shape how we react to being placed in particular situations.

As soon as Student 1, who happened to be a male, raised this question, I immediately felt honored and respected. I thought to myself, "This student not only sees me, but is verbally expressing that he sees me." Many of my white students distance themselves from race-based discussions while claiming to be color-blind, a notion which serves to treat "race as an irrelevant, invisible, and taboo topic" (Howard, 2006, p. 57); therefore, it was refreshing to entertain the honesty, directness, and boldness embodied in this student's initial question.

Of course, I never know exactly how these spontaneous conversations will turn out, but, comparatively speaking, I considered the above conversation to be nothing short of successful, informative, and culturally relevant. I quickly assessed that the initial question was absolutely authentic in motive and content. I ascertained that Student 1, though cautious, was exceptionally curious and perhaps even a bit uneasy about my comfort level as the only person of color in the entire town. The act of assessing the underlying meaning of this student's initial question helped me to avoid making unnecessary assumptions; additionally, it opened a passageway for me to remain consciously objective and reflective as I attempted to process likely implications or intentions related to his question. For example, I could have easily become suspicious by assuming that he was testing me just to see how I would react. Perhaps he wondered whether I would get upset, anxious, or angry? I could have also become defensive by thinking that he was trying to be covertly unwelcoming. Was this his way of saying I really wasn't welcome there? Was this a way of saying he was only tolerating me because he had to? I could even have taken the question as a warning that since I was the only person of color in town, perhaps I should take precautions to protect myself in case there happened to be someone lurking around who might try to hurt me.

Given my inclination to hear ideas contrary to my own, I processed this student's question and geared myself toward helping him to help me to understand his motives. After breaking down the initial tension with humor, I became ecstatic, even somewhat humbled, about the elevated level of participation that followed. As more students joined in the discussion, it became increasingly apparent that, except for one student, everyone in the class shared the same cultural background. The ensuing dialogue enriched us all as we each dared to reveal intimate slices of our lives for all to hear. The beauty of the overall process rested in an awakening, which culminated after the student–teacher dialogue. Once I posed the question relative to how our conversation might pertain to their own classes, the students constructed their individual ideas and came to terms with the need to turn the tides of their thinking. In essence, the processes I chose to employ led to a lucrative exchange that potentially propelled my students to become considerably more culturally sensitive.

The following exchange, which I will refer to as Dialogue #2, reveals issues pertaining to race, culture, and stereotypes. In comparison to Dialogue #1, the atmosphere around the initial questioning began on a much lighter note while exploring the use of music in the classroom.

Dialogue #2

Student 1: We can't move like you because we're just regular white people. (*Initial comment*)
Teacher: And I'm just a regular black person! (*Humor*) What are you guys talking about? (*Assessing underlying meanings*)
Students: That's what we mean . . . regular black people move like you!
Teacher: What are you saying about the way I move! (*Assessing underlying meanings, inviting conversation*)
Student 1: You've got rhythm.
Student 2: Yeah, and soul . . . we look "white" when we try to do the song and steps.
Teacher: Okay, let me get this straight. Are you guys saying that compared to me, you don't look as good doing the moves because you're white and I'm black? (*Reframing questions for clarity*)
Students: (Laughter) Yes!!!

Teacher: You guys are full of it!!! So, according to you, that means that any black person in the world could come in here and do the moves better than you! This also means that no white person in the world could do the moves better than I! (*Probing for more information*)

Student 3: Pretty much . . . Maybe not in the whole world; there might be one or two white people who could move as well as you!

Teacher: Okay, let's stop a minute. Think about three white people you know that move well, dance well, or have a very good sense of rhythm.

Students: Justin Timberlake . . . the music teacher at my school . . . Ginger Rogers . . . Lady GaGa . . . my daughters. [The list became quite extensive.]

Teacher: So would you agree that there may be more than just one or two white people who could do these moves just as well as I?

Students: Yeah, guess so.

Teacher: Now, try to think of three black people you know that do not move well.

Student 5: There was a boy in my class who couldn't move well but it was because he had balance issues, but he was the only black kid in my class who didn't move well!

Student 6: Can't think of any . . . never seen any black person who didn't move well . . . all the black people I know can really move.

Teacher: Then, could it be that you think all black people have a "good" sense of rhythm because you haven't met or seen any without it? (*Questioning for clarification*)

Students: Maybe. But are there really black people without rhythm?

Teacher: Let's think about it like this. There are people in all races that have different senses or styles of rhythm. Rather than using the term good or bad sense of rhythm, let's think about it in terms of diverse senses of rhythm. So, if that's the case, yes, there are black people who do not have the same sense of rhythm that I have. Now let's take what we've just talked about and think about why this may be significant in our classrooms. (*Reframing for clarity*)

Student 1: It's about student expectations. If we think all black kids have rhythm, we may have false expectations. Like I used to think all black kids liked to dance.

Student 3: But it's just hard to believe that all black people don't have rhythm. So, I've got to be careful with putting my black kids on the spot. I think they should always be the ones to model the movements we do in class. One time, one of my black kids didn't get the movements right away, and I got upset because I thought the movements should have come natural to him! Talking about a disconnect!

Teacher: I think you're getting the hang of it. As teachers, we must be very careful to avoid stereotypical thinking about our students based on race or culture!

Unlike Dialogue #1, a sea of unstoppable laughter initiated by the students themselves accompanied the Dialogue #2; therefore, I didn't really need to create a situation to deliberately insert humor. Admittedly, the students not only laughed at themselves as they tried to mimic my movements, but they also laughed at their own insistence that their "whiteness" prevented them from giving the movements justice. Of course, I couldn't help but laugh with them, but it was important that I make the leap toward analyzing the stereotypical statements that had just taken place about race. Upon asking them to think of three white people who move well, the laughter dissipated gradually as I invited them into a reflective space, which served as an opportunity to probe for new information. I think they surprised themselves at how spontaneously they were able to come up with names of white people who moved well; however, most of them insisted that the white people they named moved well because they were not "regular" white people. As we deepened the discussion toward blacks who didn't move well, the tone quickly shifted to one of total seriousness, and interestingly enough, most of the responses were directed to students in their classrooms. I was more than pleased to observe the direction of this seamless transition as it made my job much easier. Without much additional probing, the students began to make important connections between their stereotypical notions and the missteps that might result in the classroom. Again, I was pleasantly satisfied with the results.

There is more than enough work to do around issues of race, class, and culture, and as an African American professor from the south teaching mostly white students, I feel that I have been blessed to pour morsels of knowledge into the minds of my students—morsels that have the potential to morph into substantive and lasting quantities of cultural sensitivity such that every child will feel honored, valued, and loved. Morsels such as continuous, introspective dialogue disbands barriers of fear and confusion; the translucence of transparency tramples the opaqueness of silence; transformations in thought gradually replace normalcy of the status quo; and we dare to begin a new dance—stepping lightly into the galaxy of respect, equality, and freedom!

Questions for Reflection

1. The author mentions four processes that help her to address student questions and comments pertaining to race, culture, and class. Which of these processes appeal to you? Which of these processes does not appeal

to you? Think about your responses and the meanings associated with your responses.

2. In what ways have you prepared yourself to address student questions pertaining to race, culture, and/or class? Describe a situation in which such questions have come up in your class and what questions it raised for you.

3. If you are a white teacher with primarily white students, how do you prepare to address and encourage student questions about race, culture, and class?

References

Boyd, B. (2004). Laughter and literature: A play theory of humor and literature. *Philosophy and Literature, 28*(1), 1–22.

Feistinger, L. (1957). *A theory of cognitive dissonance*. Palo Alto, CA: Stanford University Press.

Freire, P. (1970). *Pedagogy of the oppressed*. New York, NY: Herder and Herder.

Howard, G. (2006). *We can't teach what we don't know*. New York, NY: Teachers College Press.

Rogers, C. (1951). *Client-centered therapy: Its current practice, implications, and theory*. Boston, MA: Houghton-Mifflin.

Schaffer, N. (1981). *The art of laughter*. New York: Columbia University Press.

Schmidt, N. E., & Williams, D. I. (1971). The evolution of theories of humor. *Journal of Behavioral Science, 1*, 95–106.

Section III

Practice in Community

8 Culturally Responsive Professional Practices in the College Classroom and Professional Sites

Marjorie A. Jones

Throughout the life span, every individual is teaching and learning, engaging in the process by which we learn and develop. Many factors intersect in giving and receiving information. One of those factors is culture. As an educator, being reflective of the impact of one's own culture in the teaching/learning encounter is critical in facilitating an optimal interchange and exchange of information. Familiarity with the culture of one's students is instructive to the educator as she determines curriculum, classroom climate, teacher–learner relationship, and the pedagogical strategies that the she will employ to engage students. This is not only appropriate in the classroom, but in all professions that require culturally responsive professional practices.

Teacher preparation and human services programs at Lesley University are conducted through a variety of delivery models, among diverse populations, and in a variety of geographical settings. All of these variables must be considered when engaging in culturally responsive professional practices. Students from across the United States and several countries of the world study on the university's Cambridge campus in Massachusetts, a hub of intellectual and social activities. Though the majority of the faculty and students have some common cultural experiences, it is still critical to consider aspects of culture as faculty and students interface with each other. Faculty teach across Massachusetts and in other states within the United States. In some settings, the faculty member is visitor or outsider and must gain an appreciation of local culture as they engage with students in students' local environments. In yet another program design, faculty teach in countries outside the United States, and students from countries outside the United States come to the Cambridge campus for instruction. This latter program delivery structure challenges faculty based in the United States to practice the concept of cultural humility as they engage with students from cultures different from their own, as learning about culture is a lifelong activity. Though intellectual, technological, and other teaching-learning resources may be more abundant and available in the U.S., faculty who engage with students who come from settings where these resources are limited must accept that faculty continue to be both teacher and learner, and must empower the learner to consider himself/herself as knower and creator of knowledge, particularly in issues that relate to cultural experiences.

This chapter shares my experiences as a faculty member born outside of the United States, a naturalized U.S. citizen, and teaching at Lesley University for twenty years. I was born in Guyana, South America, a former British colony whose history reflected slavery and indentureship. By the 1960s the ethnic groups that had experienced slavery and indentureship were now represented in leadership roles in all strata of the society. At age nineteen I migrated, in January, to the United States of America to attend a historically black college in Ohio. The United States was experiencing the height of the Civil Rights Movement. I did not understand why my brilliant, gifted classmates were putting their studies on hold to go to other states to participate in marches and boycotts. This began my introduction into understanding the various nuances of race and culture that impact specifically my, but everyone's lived experiences. Through these experiences I began reflecting on and exploring my own understanding of my identity and impact of sociocultural realities within the United States of America.

I have spent my entire career in the profession of education teaching at the secondary level and in higher education in teacher preparation programs. I have facilitated workshops for professionals in a variety of community-based education and human services organizations in the United States, Guyana, and the Caribbean.

Understanding and reflecting on one's own culture is an important exercise for all who engage in providing professional services. Self-reflection was important for me, having spent my formative years in a culture outside of the U.S. This acknowledgment was important as I engaged students in reflecting on their cultural experiences as they interacted with students who, in a majority of cases, came from cultures different from their own. Appreciating the influences that have contributed to the formation of one's cultural identity gives opportunity for understanding self and self in the context of others, especially those whose cultural identity is different from one's own.

This chapter reflects on the preparation and professional experiences of two populations who serve in diverse contexts. One population comprises classroom teachers who have had two to three years of being responsible for a classroom after completing an undergraduate preservice teacher education program at Lesley University. They reflect on the ways in which the university classroom content and field placement experiences prepared them to engage in culturally responsive professional practices. The classroom teachers, of European descent, work in culturally diverse field placement sites. They consider how they navigate aspects of race, ethnicity, language, and socioeconomic status as they provide instruction in the classroom.

The second population comprises a group of graduate trained human service professionals who have been engaged in their various professions from three to five years and are providing professional services in the areas of domestic violence, probation services, and school welfare in Guyana, South America. These Guyanese human services professionals participated in a graduate program that met in Cambridge, Massachusetts and Georgetown, Guyana over a two-year period. Two of the thirteen participants had visited the United States prior to their graduate study.

The Guyanese students, though working in their own home country, were challenged when they were asked to reflect on the ways in which aspects of diversity—specifically related to geography (urban/rural), religion, and ethnicity—impacted their professional practices. It may seem obvious that the U.S. classroom teachers should be critically reflective that their professional practices reflect culturally responsive professional practices; however the Guyanese human service providers, though sharing similar nationality and sociocultural realities as their clients, needed to reflect on their own cultural identities as they engaged with clients whose ethnicity, geography, and religion impacted the ways in which the service provider could engage with the clients.

The United States is becoming more racially, ethnically, and linguistically diverse than ever, a trend that is expected to continue well into the twenty-first century (Villegas & Lucas, 2001, p. 3). As a result, the population in classrooms is also becoming more diverse. To respond to the changing student population in elementary and secondary schools, teacher education programs will need to reconsider the content of the established preservice curriculum (Villegas & Lucas, 2001, p. 25). Successful teachers need more than competence in subject area knowledge. Acknowledging and understanding culture, of both teacher and student, is an essential foundation for teaching and learning. Villegas and Lucas propose several strands for preparing culturally responsive teachers, which include gaining sociocultural consciousness, developing an affirming attitude towards students from culturally diverse backgrounds, learning about students and their communities, and cultivating culturally responsive teaching practices. Darling-Hammond and Bransford consider aspects of diversity including culture and racial/ethnic origins, language, economic status, and learning challenges (Darling-Hammond & Bransford, 2005).

The Teacher Education Program

During each of the four years of the undergraduate education program at Lesley University, aspiring teachers take courses that address both historical and contemporary issues in education coupled with field experiences that provide a laboratory for professional practices. Preparing preservice teachers to engage in culturally responsive practices requires that faculty engage students in the college classroom with the theory of culturally responsive professional practices in a safe and nonjudgmental forum for exploration of those theories and their impact on the lives of the preservice teachers, their students, and the communities in which they will work. Course content is not culture-neutral, hence the importance of discussions and reflections between faculty and students, and students and students in the college classroom. The courses discussed here are the ones that focus specifically on exploring both teacher and student diversity and the culturally responsive professional practices required in classroom settings.

During the first year, students enroll in Teaching, Learning and Social Responsibility, a course that introduces aspiring teachers to the historical and contemporary role of the school in a multicultural society, paying attention to the social realities of teachers and students in the school's culture. The preservice teachers consider the variety of ways in which teachers' and students' sociocultural realities either promote or derail the process of establishing and maintaining a teaching/learning environment that promotes the total development of all students. In this first course, based on the work of De Rosa and Johnson (2003) students reflect on their own color, culture, class, character, and context. The benefit of beginning with this exploration is noted in a teacher's reflection:

> I never thought of culture before, especially my culture. I didn't know how to describe my culture but this was a helpful activity because I began to see that I could not take everything for granted and understand that to develop a positive teacher–student relationship I would have to think about who I am and who my students are.

In the second year, students enroll in Characteristics of Children with Special Needs to begin an examination of instruction cognizant of the needs of students with physical, social, and emotional disabilities. An understanding of the necessary collaboration between special education and general education is critical so that an inclusionary education can be offered to a range of students. One of the areas of awareness that students note is that responsive professional practices benefit all students.

Meeting the Individual Needs of Diverse Populations, offered in year three, provides exposure to the broadest definition of diversity. Definitions include consideration of race, ethnicity, sex, age, physical and mental ability, sexual orientation, religion, work and family status, weight and appearance and other aspects of identity. The course provides an integrated study of the learner, the learning situation and the learning process in diverse environments. It has as its vision the words of Lisa Delpit, "Until we can see the world as others see it, all the educational reforms in the world will come to naught" Lisa Delpit (2006, 134).

Teachers need to consider and integrate a number of factors that impact teaching and learning. These factors should be reflected in the content of the college curriculum, paying attention to both readiness of students and relevancy to their developmental needs, the pedagogical strategies that are used, and a consideration of the different ways in which students learn. Critical consideration should be given to the geographic community, the school, the classroom, the students, and their families.

In year four students enroll in a Sheltered English Instruction course, which focuses on teaching students whose first language is not English. As members of a global community, the need to build competency and fluency in languages and increase our knowledge of various cultures becomes more evident in the practice of culturally responsive professional practices.

One teacher reflected:

> I believe that the course, Meeting the Individual Needs of Diverse Learners has equipped me the most to respond with cultural competence. If it wasn't for that course I feel as if I may not have been prepared coming into my current job . . . I took the Sheltered English Immersion course that I feel helped me become further equipped to teach students from different cultures . . . different backgrounds . . . as well as language difference. My student teaching and my practicum also provided me with experience with students from different cultures . . .

University coursework can be quite effective, if properly conceived and delivered in presenting theoretical frameworks and research principles that support innovative practices (DeVillar, Faltis, & Cummins, 1994, p. 109). Methodology courses afford experiences in modeling appropriate professional practices. The relative ineffectiveness of theory alone, in the absence of concrete demonstrations and/or practice sessions, is supported by research on in-service teacher training (DeVillar et al., 1994, p. 109). K–12 students' reflections on their schooling experiences invariably include reflections on their relationships with their teachers, which are instructive to the success of teaching and learning. In the college classroom students benefit from engagement with others who are seeking to build levels of awareness and understanding about working in diverse environments. Appropriate field experiences provide opportunities to observe, participate in classroom instruction, and reflect, both with current practitioners and then with peers in the classroom, on the experiential aspects of culturally responsive professional practices.

Table 8.1 Demographics and Diversity of a 5th Grade Classroom of Twenty-Four Students in Boston, MA

Category	# of students
IEP	0
English Lang. Dev. Level 1	1
English Lang. Dev. Level 3	3
English Lang. Dev. Level 4 & 5 combined	9
Hispanic	13
Black	7
Vietnamese	4
Muslim	1
Christian	23

Source: Russell Elementary School, Boston, MA.

Teachers in this study noted the following areas as significant in their preparation to be effective classroom teachers and also as areas that should continually be reinforced throughout teacher preparation.

- class management
- conducting parent conferences
- communicating with parents who speak a language other than English
- more familiarity with the content of individualized education programs (IEPs) and strategies for responding
- transitioning from theory to practice
- raising cultural awareness and cultural acceptance
- counseling children as a teacher
- strategies for responding to "bad behavior"

Diversity is a reality in classrooms, as reflected in the demographics and diversity of a 5th grade classroom of twelve male and twelve female students in Boston, MA (see Table 8.1).

Reflections on Professional Practices

Lesley graduates and other school personnel identified the following six areas as examples where teachers lacked the requisite knowledge and attitude to engage in culturally responsive professional practices.

1. Family composition. Some teachers had a fixed and limited definition of family and were unfamiliar with the student's concept of "living as a family," which could mean that grandparents and other relatives could be present in the home and that a male uncle who resided in the home

was the "father figure." "While some live in traditional two parent families, many others live in extended families, in blended families, or with non-parental caregivers (such as grandparents, godparents or aunts and uncles)" (Suarez, Suarez-Orozco, & Todorva, 2008, p. 36).

2. Materialism. Some teachers question why a family would purchase certain items for their children and may ridicule the child for having the item by noting "how can you afford that?" The family, on the other hand, sees the purchase of the item as being able to identify with having economic resources and resembling a more "mainstream" position in society.

3. Language. There seems to be a higher value placed on French than Spanish and a lesser value on Haitian Creole and nonstandard English. Such value assignments on languages seem to distance teachers from students.

> Children operate on several levels in their use of language (dialect, slang, street-language), which can result in their inability to consistently engage the language of the classroom. Teachers can use the classroom community to both inform themselves and support students in navigating the use of the various 'types of language' as students build competence in the use of the language of the classroom.
> (Suarez-Orozco and Suaraz-Orozco, 2001, p. 73)

4. Cultural capital. Because of the neighborhoods in which the families reside and the jobs they hold, some teachers are unable to recognize the social capital that the families and students bring.

5. Cultural schizophrenia. One teacher's view: the Vietnamese child is too quiet. The Hispanic child is too loud.

> The teacher–student relationship is critical to both effective teaching and effective learning. Understanding the culture of one's students promotes an appreciation of who they are and encourages the teacher to explore the best ways to engage them in the classroom. Students' motivation and effort in school require a meaningful connection between student and teacher.
> (Suarez et al., 2008, p. 44)

6. Communication. One school administrator noted that some white teachers perceive communication as a "Ping Pong" game—each person taking his/her turn one at a time and in order—while the diverse student body may view communication as a "Volley Ball" game where a player could get into the game as needed. Some teachers see this behavior as a cultural deficit.

The Lesley/Guyana Program

In Guyana, and in many developing countries, violence against women and children is endemic. The degree program aimed to build the capacity of human service professionals to respond to the needs of traumatized youth, families, and communities. The culture of Guyana is influenced by the historical experiences of the "six peoples" that historically comprised the Guyanese population (African, Amerindian, Chinese, East Indian, European, and Portuguese). Access to mental health resources is significantly different among the urban, rural, and hinterland populations.

An independent republic since 1966, Guyana continues to devise new and relevant ways to respond to the needs of its diverse population, balancing some "older" cultural practices with "new" ways of upholding the rights of all individuals, particularly women and children. This struggle is influenced by the easy access to Western culture through travel and the media, which must often be balanced with the availability of resources locally, and the national culture. An atmosphere of violence impacts the psyche of adults, youth, and children and, therefore, impacts the work that is undertaken by educators and human services providers such as the Lesley University graduates.

Guyanese Students Reflections on Cultural Learning

The Guyanese students reflected on their own cultural learning based on the experiences of the workshops they designed and facilitated as the final activity of their Lesley/Guyana program. The following are reflections from several students:

> We serve a diverse population in the various regions and it was stated as an example that a person of a different racial or ethnic identity might be uncomfortable working with a service provider who is of a different group . . . I have experienced whereby due to my ethnicity I am relegated to a specific political orientation . . . in the past, I was angry and hurt at this type of behavior but we need to remain professional and let the person know we respect their choice . . . I felt personally angry at women for what I thought to be weakness and stupidity especially Indo-Guyanese women for staying in abusive relationships.
>
> (Male)

> There has definitely been a major shift in my views on culture and people since the exercise of reflection on the impact of culture on my own

life. I see my own multicultural strengths as acceptance, being nonjudgmental, tolerance and receptiveness.

(Female)

It is the perception of African teachers that the Indian teachers cannot
deal with the African students in terms of discipline. Most of the African teachers believe that the other religions are inferior to their religion,
Christianity.

(Male)

Prior to the workshop I attempted to become culturally competent in
order to relate to all participants and remove some of the preconceptions
and biases I may have had also due to the information filtered to me
before working in the community.

(Female)

Guyanese have a culture where parents and adults respond to children
in an authoritative manner . . . persons usually find it difficult to accept
children as having their own individualization in the sense of a child
being able to make certain decisions. As a consequence, persons within
the Guyanese society may experience difficulties understanding and
accepting the personality traits of truants. They would respond to this as
the parents are not strong and you need to deal with the parents, not the
child/children.

(Female)

Guyanese Practitioners' Reflections on Culturally Responsive Professional Practices

Guyana, a developing nation, is experiencing some of the challenges experienced in developed nations, but it lacks both personnel and material resources
to respond adequately to the challenges. The Lesley program has added significantly to the knowledge, skills, and awareness of the graduates who, with
skill and confidence, have begun to explore their own cultural realities so that
they might respond appropriately to the cultural diversity present among the
Guyanese population.

Irish and Scrubbs (2012), reflecting on the importance of understanding
cultural practices, note that every student possesses a unique cultural background, which involves various traditions, norms, and values that inform ways
of knowing and learning. This consideration of traditions practiced by an

individual extends to some families and communities. One of the Guyanese students shared the following experience.

> One of my key functions . . . is to address attendance and punctuality in schools. Through my investigations . . . I figured out that in a certain riverine Amerindian area, attendance in schools on Mondays is less than 4%. When I went into the area to conduct community tours, I was told by parents that Monday is market day . . . and the whole family would go to market . . . the parents related that since they were children their parents used to take them on Mondays to market so they are doing the same with their children. Normally, I would create a system to charge these parents for neglecting to send their children to school but after understanding that this is a cultural issue, I changed my approach and so a series of meetings were held . . . to sensitize parents about the importance of education for their children.
>
> (Male)

Understanding cultural practices suggests that engaging in ethnographic studies of communities may provide specific information about the cultural practices that reflect deeply held values of an individual or community. Some cultural practices involve the folkways practiced by a group. Folkways reflect an intimate connection with one's identity. At times some folkways are not easily explained, but they are revered, practiced, and passed down through generations. The scenario described by the student reflects a cultural practice strictly observed by a family and community that was unfamiliar to the service provider even though the service provider had been working in the community for several years. As professionals provide direct service to individuals, the focus commonly is on responding to the articulated need of the client. It is important, however, to acknowledge that a particular need can be reflective of needs, experiences, and norms in the family, community, religious practices, geography, or other contextual factors.

Conclusion

Identity and culture are a part of every individual's reality. Every individual does not often engage in self-reflection and projection of the impact of one's identity and culture on one's professional practices. Curriculum in teacher education programs that includes content and experiences related to culture, both in the college classroom and practicum sites, provides opportunities for discussion of individual cultural experiences and the cultural experiences of the school population that help prepare preservice teachers to develop and practice professional competencies, taking into account the diversity of the U.S. school population. Such a curriculum allows preservice teachers to address fears and apprehensions about working in communities different from their own, and allows explorations of culturally responsive professional practices.

The responses of Guyanese professionals highlighted the fact that all professionals must continually reflect on their own cultural experiences in the context of providing services to their clients. Guyanese professionals who had served in their professional capacities for three to five years developed a new understanding of culturally competent professional practices when they considered their own cultural experiences and the ways in which ethnicity, religion, folkways, and geography impacted how they engage and support their clients.

In my initial experiences at Lesley University, there were students who questioned the need for courses that addressed aspects of cultural diversity. Though I was convinced that there was a critical need, my response was first to consider how I would interact with students, then consider why students would be resistant to that area of studies and explore ways in which I would engage the students in exploring identity of self and "other" so that they might note the benefits of learning about cultures different from their own. One critical exercise was to allow each student to present his or her culture to note that each of us come from a cultural experience, and these experiences impact the ways in which teachers and students engage with each other in the classroom and as human service providers seek to provide services to their constituents.

Questions for Reflection

1. Teacher preparation programs must provide preservice teachers with information about the demographics of school populations. How can this information be embedded in both the college classroom content and the experiences in practicum sites to promote culturally competent professional practices?
2. How are your expectations of student knowledge and achievement impacted by the larger designations of countries into "first-world" and "third-world" categories, race and ethnicity, and geographical locations of schools?
3. Acknowledging cultural practices of clients is critical in providing client-friendly services. How can language be framed to honor cultural practices while encouraging consideration of best practices in professional practices?
4. What strategies can professionals employ to prepare themselves when providing service in cultures different from their own (consider aspects of geography, language, parenting styles, religion, etc.)?

References

Darling-Hammond, L., & Bransford, J. (Eds.). (2005). *Preparing teachers for a changing world.* San Francisco, CA: Jossey-Bass.

Delpit, L. (2006). *Other people's children: Cultural conflict in the classroom.* New York, NY: New Press.

DeRosa, P., and Johnson, U. (2003). *The 10 Cs: A Model of Diversity Awareness and Social Change.* Randolph, MA: Changeworks Consulting.

DeVillar, R. A., Faltis, C. J., & Cummins, J. P., eds. (1994). *Cultural diversity in schools: From rhetoric to practice.* New York, NY: State University of New York Press.

Irish, C. and Scrubb, M. (2012). *Five competencies for culturally competent teaching and learning.* Faculty Focus Magna Publisher.

Suarez-Orozco, C., & Suarez-Orozco, M. (2001). *Children of immigration.* Cambridge, MA: Harvard University Press.

Suarez-Orozco, C., Suarez-Orozco, M., & Todorva, I. (2008). *Learning a new land: Immigrant students in American society.* Cambridge, MA: The Belknap Press of Harvard University Press.

Villegas, A. M., & Lucas, T. (2001). *Educating culturally competent teachers: A coherent approach.* Albany, NY: SUNY Press.

9 Adult Learners

Where I'm From and Why It Matters

Deborah D. Wright

All the world is my school and all humanity is my teacher.
—George Whitman

Administrator by day, adjunct faculty by night, I originally started teaching when I was an admissions counselor enrolling adult students who were returning to college. It was my attempt to "hang on" to them longer after having bonded with them during the admissions process. I wanted to ensure that they had a smooth transition as they returned to college.

One observation that I made regularly on the first night of class was the "deer in the headlight" look on the students' faces as I stopped in to visit. It was on most of their faces and evident in all of the classes that I visited. The full comprehension of that look would not register until later in my teaching career.

While the orientation class is only one of several courses that I have taught, it remains one of my favorites. I enjoy this class immensely and have continued to introduce and teach some version of it at several different institutions. It was while teaching at Lesley University and after attending the Cultural Literacy Curriculum Institute (CLCI) that I started putting all the pieces together to really glean the significance of the look that I described earlier. During the Institute I discovered the assignment by Linda Christensen titled "Where I'm From: Inviting Students' Lives into the Classroom." Kentucky's 2015–2016 poet laureate, George Ella Lyon, created the poem at the heart of the assignment. She also has published a book titled *Where I'm From: Where Poems Come From*. As she describes the evolution of her list of people, objects, and memories that eventually became the poem, she also acknowledges that the "list form is simple and familiar, and the question of where you are from reaches deep" (Lyon, 1993).

The poetry assignment lingered with me throughout the Institute, although it was only a small part of a very full agenda. I remember thinking how appropriate creating such a poem would be for my adult students. I had no idea of the impact it would make as I introduced the activity into my next class.

The exercise itself, as Linda Christensen describes, is designed "to find ways to make students feel significant and cared about as well as to find space for their lives to become part of the curriculum" (Christensen, 1998). This certainly describes my adult students who often feel unworthy of a second chance and feel that, short of validation from a college transcript, they have nothing of academic value to offer.

We were encouraged to take actionable lessons from the Institute and transform our classes. I introduced this assignment the next semester in my orientation course. The first day of class, students had completed the preliminary introductions, which included using three words to describe how they were feeling about returning to school. (The three words—scared, anxious, and excited—generally rise to the top of the list.)

Then I shared with them Lyon's poetry from the exercise. She begins each stanza with "I'm from," followed by images, people, memories, smells, sounds. We discussed what they thought it revealed about the author, and what kind of images she used. Her poem can be found on her website.

After the students got over the initial puzzlement of why we were reading poetry and what connection this could have with the course, the transition from guesswork to analysis began. We moved from the literal interpretations of "She's from the South, she lives in the country, and she goes to church" to more complex "I think what she is trying to say is" and "when I read this it makes me feel . . . " Now they were almost all thinking, "How would I tell *my* story?"

I have them complete the "Where I'm From" assignment and bring the completed poem to read out loud and share with the class the following week. Although this assignment does provide a glimpse into the students' writing abilities, the assignment was certainly not meant to prematurely intimidate or challenge anyone so early into the course schedule. So I was astonished the following week to pick up whispered snippets of conversations as I entered the classroom that morning.

"This assignment was really difficult!" confided one student to another. "I started and stopped three times before I got anything on paper," confessed another.

What in the world is going on, I wondered to myself, thinking that I had somehow made an error on the syllabus or miscommunicated what was due. I had purposely designed the course to be progressively more demanding, and given that this was only the start of week two, we were all going to be in a world of trouble! Not wanting to encourage more of what I perceived as complaining from the students, I jumped right in by asking who was ready and wanted to be the first to share their poem. The class got quiet as heads turned left, right, and down. Slowly, a few hesitant hands extended into the air.

For the next two and a half hours I sat stunned as I listened to deeply personal stories and reflections from students who seemingly chose the most difficult memories of their lives to share and benchmark their identity. In this moment, I could tell by their reactions that the students were also deeply moved by the level of sharing; each person seemed bolstered by the previous story to open up even more with the explanation of their words, if not by the words themselves.

Given permission to use the stories, here are excerpts from a few of the students:

I am From

—By MC

> *Where I'm From*
> *Mustard on Coney's and salt potatoes*
> *A childhood chronicled by comic books*
> *Provided in return for a moment of silence*
> *Reality was never so engulfing*

> *Where I'm From*
> *Home sick at Grandma's again*
> *Life size statue of the Virgin Mary in the backyard*
> *Though I've discarded the doctrine*
> *Music will more than bridge the gap*

Hands

—By DZ

> *I am from that one look that brings me back to my still place.*
> *That one look that burns right through my flesh.*
> *That one look that controls my whole being.*

> *I am from do it yourself or it won't get done.*

> *I am from unknown chances of open and closed hands.*
> *Hands that often met cheeks.*

Cheeks that allowed my tongue to roll with lies just so that she would not get the blame.

I am from hands that never failed to protect.
Hands that forced respect.

I am from a long walk

—By JM

I am from a long walk
Two leaps and a jump
Falling into trusted arms
A place called home

I am from a green eye
A crooked smile
A first love
And dark skin

Needless to say, after listening to the first three or four students struggle to even read through their presentations, I finally understood the earlier comments about how difficult this assignment was for them. By lunchtime and about fifteen students later, there wasn't a dry eye in the classroom.

These are *my* students. The adults I often challenge colleagues to carve out a space for in their syllabus and to actively include in our classrooms. These students are not just from the United States but from all over the world, and many of them bring with them weighty baggage covered with stickers that reveal fears, doubts, disappointment, and pain. They also carry stories— some happy ones and many sad ones. What I discovered that day by listening to their stories and watching their interactions with each other was that all their steps had been ordered to bring them to this place, on this day, at this time. And that bringing who they were as "adult learners" was as significant and as much a part of them as their culture, language, or ethnicity. These stories were coming with them whether I acknowledged them or not. And not allowing their stories would have deprived me, and the rest of the class, of the trusting and intimate journey that we had just embarked upon.

Culture, described by authors Iris Varner and Linda Beamer, "is the coherent, learned, shared view of a group of people about life's concerns, expressed in symbols and activities, that ranks what is important, furnishes attitudes about what things are appropriate, and dictates behavior" (2010, p. 10).

Having this activity in the class, as unassuming as it seemed, had just opened the door to their culture as a group of adult learners.

Malcolm Knowles summed up the state of adult learning in 1973 when he titled his book *The Adult Learner: A Neglected Species*. While adult students have moved further up the higher education ladder, it is still appropriate to examine the state of adult learning theory in the same context as other ideas of cultural significance. How do we move beyond the idea of humility, competency, curriculum, and cultural literacy to action and to change in the classroom? Learning, as reflected by Sidney Jourard, "is not a task or problem: [but] a way to be in the world. Man learns as he pursues goals and projects that have meaning for him" (1972, p. 66). How do we allow the adult student to bring the world into the classroom through our curriculum and teaching? For me, this introduced two further questions: Why is this concept important in the classroom for adult learners? As a teacher, just how do I go about "bringing the world into the classroom"?

During my lunch break I had a chance to ponder that very question. Back in my office during lunch, I thought about what had happened during this exercise. I found I was emotionally exhausted, overwhelmed, and unprepared for the level of raw emotion and disclosure that had taken place. I had unknowingly created a space for students in this classroom that was now wide open. I found myself wrestling with maintaining the space between student and faculty, between time and agenda, and between roles and humanity.

To ignore the moment would be to lessen their experiences and somehow dishonor and default on the trust. I struggled with how to be responsive to all they had revealed when there was, for me, varying degrees of experiences with which I could even identify. Did my syllabus allow room for us to continue down this road or should I just return and check off introductions on my task box and move on with the lesson? I began to focus on what each student had shared and began to note where there were commonalities with my own life. Could I remain the authority in the class if I opened up as much with them, or would my position as teacher be diminished and my ability to impart knowledge compromised?

Educators might be more inclined to address the obvious cultural differences that you see like race, religion, and gender; the idea and importance of being culturally sensitive to adults could be overlooked. The importance has to do with the idea of self-concept. Knowles explains that the first adult learner characteristic of andragogy is tied to self-concept; and that no adult learner will ever learn under conditions incongruent with his self-concept. Because of that, classes should allow for participation in self-diagnosis of educational needs, planning experiences, and developing a suitable learning climate (Knowles, 1973, p. 253). In a classroom of adult learners, this is vital.

I can say that this need for self-concept has been evidenced in my classes over and over again. When five-minute introductions become twenty-minute histories, full of validations, accomplishments, and experiences, it is clear that the need to discuss their journey is important to the students as a community of learners. From the observation I witnessed in my class with the first assignment, it was evident that even a slight adjustment in the assignment or syllabus could allow space for their stories. This is where I bridge the gap to make the connection between cultural humility and the adult learner. Often the less dominant culture is the "neglected species," and our responsibility as educators is to create an inclusive classroom, thereby extending to the adult learner the necessary and needed learning environment.

I finally decided the best way to respond to the students would be to share my own "Where I'm From" poem with the class, the one I had written during the first day of the CLCI. As an African American woman, I did not so much think of myself as privileged, but I did realize that in the students' eyes, by virtue of being the faculty, I represented authority and that placed me at an advantage in the classroom. However, what they did not know was that I am a first-generation college graduate. My father joined the military at the age of seventeen and was sent off to fight for a country that, at that time, placed little value on his existence at home. He went on to serve thirty years in the military, and I grew up moving and traveling all over the world as an army brat. They did not know that my mother attended secretarial school and did much to organize local civil rights events in Birmingham, Alabama. I shared with them my story. Our journeys led us to that shared moment where we allowed room for each other's experiences as a part of all of our personal growth.

Where I'm From

—By D. Wright

> I am from red clay dirt,
> From fried chicken, ribs, and
> Macaroni and cheese that would bring tears to your eyes.
>
> I am from slamming screen doors,
> From hand fans and flies,
> From daredevil country cousins and sweaty aunts with smothering hugs.
> I am from relatives who are strangers and all have pictures
> Of Jesus, JFK, and MLK hanging on their walls.

I am from foreign accents and languages
From snitzel, pomme fritz and Oktoberfest;
From "Can I touch your hair?
Your skin, your soul?"

I am from soldiers, always soldiers
Marching, saluting, waving, daring, dying. . .
I am from tanks, M16's, 45's, Humvees and Huey's
From exchange rates that move faster than a BMW on the autobahn.

I am from travel, family and introductions every two years to those
I love
"Hello Granny, yes I remember you."
After fifteen minutes the strangers are gone.
I am from family again.

The response to my openness with the students led to my "aha" moment in the classroom. Cultural humility is a way of not only being sensitive to others, but about being vulnerable with yourself. It was only clear to me in hindsight that what I had done was so valuable to establishing that sense of trust and humility. Presenting my story and answering their questions as a participant in the exercise, I reinforced a comfort that they were already feeling from our introductions. And this did not make me any less the professor; if anything, it solidified my position to the point that we were able to move beyond maintaining just that relationship alone.

As faculty we may feel that we need to be elevated, either consciously or unconsciously, in the classroom; that may happen professionally, academically, or emotionally, but it can create a distance that permeates into our actions, conversations, and body language. When we teach, we feel obligated to "impart knowledge" and thus must maintain this elevated status. What I experienced is that, especially with adult students, giving myself permission to be a participant in the learning process in the classroom and being emotionally available helped me to reach my students far more. It also provided an opportunity for them to be open to learning rather than feeling like they should already know everything simply because they were adults.

I started this essay as a reflection of some real challenges I was having with some of the organizational structures in my institution that were keeping me from meeting the needs of the adult students in my program. Participating in this writing helped me to recognize and understand that the concept of culture applies equally to a population of adult learners as to any other descriptive quality, such as race or ethnicity.

From one who admittedly is a passionate advocate for adult learners, I am very interested in ensuring that higher education institutions don't only think about increased enrollment numbers when they think about recruiting adult students; but that they also care to embrace and meet the needs of the non-traditional learner in a manner that includes the classroom experience. I hope that faculty see these students in their classrooms and feel a sense of responsibility and ask the question "How do I reach this student?" The key is being culturally responsive in your teaching, which can be as simple as understanding the "enormous power of listening to one's students, and willingness to be open to new learning about their hidden capabilities" (Dallalfar, Kingston-Mann, & Sieber, 2011, p. 9).

Questions for Reflection

1. Consider your current classes. How have you created inclusive space in your curriculum for the students' cultures?
2. As a faculty member, how much opportunity is there in your classrooms for students to develop their self-concept as described by Malcolm Knowles?
3. When you teach a group of students, do you relinquish or uphold your position of privilege in the classroom? What is the impact of the position of privilege you hold?

References

Christensen, L. (1998). Inviting students' lives into the classroom. *Rethinking Schools Online, 12*(2), 22–23.

Dallalfar, A., Kingston-Mann, E., & Sieber, T. (2011). *Transforming classroom culture: Inclusive pedagogical practices.* New York, NY: Palgrave MacMillan.

Jourard, S. M. (1972). Fascination: A phenomenological perspective on independent learning. In Silberman, et al. *The psychology of open teaching and learning.* Boston: Little, Brown.

Knowles, M. (1973). *The adult learner: A neglected species.* American Society for Training and Development. Houston, TX: Gulf Publishing.

Lyon, G. E. (1993). *Where I'm from.* Retrieved from http://www.georgeellalyon.com/where.html

Lyon, G. E. (1999). *Where I'm from: Where poems come from.* New York: Absey and Co.

Varner, I., & Beamer, L. (2010). *Intercultural communication in the global workplace* (5th ed.). New York: McGraw-Hill Education.

10 Working With the Self, Walking With Another

Deborah Spragg

The men and the women in the group were equally skilled. They worked with ease, with confidence, and with a playful inventiveness. No longer the "expressive therapy experts," my colleague and I marveled as the silence in the room deepened, and the concentration, the sure familiarity of our students' own expertise, held sway. The students were on their own ground. This was an unexpected and magical moment.

In July of 2013, a group of thirteen Guyanese students came to Cambridge, Massachusetts, from their homeland in order to study at Lesley University, where they were enrolled in a low-residency master's program in counseling and trauma studies. In the expressive therapies course I was teaching that summer, these impressive students, all professional human service practitioners, investigated a range of arts materials presented to them by an art therapist colleague of mine. All of the three major cultural groups in Guyana were represented in our class group, including students of East Indian, African, and indigenous Amerindian descent.

Our students that summer attended to the different qualities of specific arts materials, and considered how these qualities might impact a client's arts-based expression and the therapeutic experience. They found some of the art materials very familiar, and some less so. Their own level of familiarity often impacted the students' assessment of the therapeutic benefit of the various materials: unfamiliar materials might offer fresh inspiration, or might alternatively raise performance anxiety. Very familiar materials could provide necessary safety and containment, or might on the other hand hamper creative responses.

A host of culturally bound assumptions, expressed through the range of therapist and client preferences, will accompany any use of materials or process in arts-based therapies. The exploration of these assumptions can help to foster an attitude of flexibility, and thereby support genuinely collaborative therapeutic work. Especially for students who may offer care in unfamiliar cultural settings, the cultivation of nondefensive, open attitudes toward one's own and other's preferences is vital preparation. In January of 2017, we will send our first cohort of Lesley expressive therapies interns into settings outside of the U.S.; the exploration of personal and cultural assumptions is a key element of their curriculum.

A Context of Cultural Humility

To engage another person with openness is the most fundamental of therapeutic tasks, a learning goal not only for those who may elect to embark on a global internship, but for every single one of our master's degree students. For counselors and expressive therapists, working effectively with difference is a matter of core professional competency. The framework of cultural humility can support the critical self-assessment required for our students to expand their capacity to meet the unfamiliar in another person.

Working with the self has long been considered intrinsic to the development of those skills necessary for walking alongside another in the role of a counselor. This "self as instrument" view has been foundational for the entire history of expressive therapist and counselor training at Lesley University. Nearly thirty years ago, Virginia Satir described the "positive use of self":

> When I am in touch with myself, my feelings, my thoughts, with what I see and hear, I am growing toward becoming a more integrated self. I am more congruent, I am more 'whole,' and I am able to make greater contact with the other person.
>
> (2000, p. 17)

Being in touch in this way requires self-exploration, and is a necessary competency that we try to support in our training. Yet the use of self relies on a kind of personal psychology that is framed by Western models of healing, involving the roles of a "client" and a "therapist." The development of cultural humility goes a step beyond, into a process of self-reflection and self-critique that challenges the bias that necessarily accompanies one's unexamined life and history. In this wider view, whether working with a person in one's home community, or in the context of a global internship, the students first acknowledge that they *have* a cultural point of view, and understand that it is in need of continual assessment. As the definition of cultural humility points out, this is a lifelong process. The person I was ten years ago is different than who I am today. Which aspects of my story I choose to privilege may also change over time. The lifelong process of developing cultural humility requires that we periodically review our own narrative, and look closely, over and over again, at where, and who, we come from.

In my most recent reflections on my own upbringing, the contrast between my family's system of values regarding racial equality, and my lived experience as a white child of two white parents in a predominately white town, came into full focus. Looking back, I could see more clearly than ever how the homogeneity in the town I grew up in had left me with the imprint of implicit racism.

My Background

I was raised in an affluent "bedroom community" in New Jersey, where many of the fathers, my own included, commuted by train to work in New York City. My father was a minister, employed as an executive on the national board of a liberal Christian denomination. He'd grown up the son of a factory boiler room engineer and was the only child in his family to attend college.

My mother was from quite a different socioeconomic background than my dad; it had never occurred to my mom that she would *not* attend college; she went on to become a physician who worked in clinic settings and later in private practice in rural New Hampshire until her retirement in the 1980s. The year my mother applied to medical school at the University of Chicago, she was admitted to the program under a quota limiting female admissions to only two per year. At the time she was unaware of this quota, but it was the institutionalization of prevalent attitudes with which she'd been all too familiar.

My parents fought for civil rights, open housing, and social justice throughout their lives. In their early marriage, they lived in an urban setting. They had begun their family on the south side of Chicago, where the neighborhood was a rich mixture of diverse cultural and ethnic backgrounds. South Congregational Church in Chicago, where my father had taken the job of pastor, rose to the challenge of true integration in the early 1940s. Along with those who'd originally made up the white majority of the congregation, this church became home to African American families in the local community, and to many Japanese families who had been forced to relocate to the neighborhood from the West Coast during World War II (often despite U.S. citizenship). My father had sought out a pastorate that would naturally be a mixture of diverse people who lived in the immediate community—a "genuine, intentional fellowship which was rooted in the neighborhood," in his own words.

In the early 1950s, after having had three kids while living in much more diverse and urban communities, my parents settled in my mother's hometown of Westfield, New Jersey. My grandmother still lived in this town of thirty thousand. My father commuted into New York, and my mother took paid positions in local Planned Parenthood clinics serving several communities of color in the surrounding area. My closest sister and I, the last of my parents' five children, were to be born in Westfield. While living there, my parents continued to work for open housing, but their values were not particularly reflected in the town as a whole. Westfield was quite a contrast with the Chicago community they'd lived in as a young family; significantly for me, it was home to very few people of color.

Proximity

Based on my family's culture, I'd always assumed my membership in the group of people that decried racial prejudice. But as the youngest of the five children, the town that *I* grew up in was primarily white and affluent. My social engagement was more informed by anti-war protests and the free school movement than by issues of racial equity. The difference between the milieus of my own upbringing and that of my eldest sibling, eleven years my senior, is illustrative of the importance of *proximity*. My eldest sister's interest in social justice issues remained a focal point throughout her life, and I believe this interest was partly secured by her membership in a fully integrated community as a child.

I joined the faculty at Lesley University full-time in 2012, after having worked as an expressive therapist in psychiatric treatment settings for many years. At Lesley, the proximity of many colleagues and administrators of very different backgrounds than mine supported fresh conversations that directly engaged the impact of my attitudes and assumptions. I remember a brief exchange in which my Assistant Dean gently opened my eyes to the circumstances that challenged the Guyanese students who had come to Lesley for their summer residency in 2013. I'd assumed that once they had returned to Guyana to complete their program requirements at home, our students could get together without any hardship involved. In actuality, they traveled two and three hours, some by boat, to meet as a group every month, while balancing highly demanding jobs (with many clients and few resources) alongside of various family commitments. The conversation with my colleague, who was both better informed and also more awake to the lives of our Guyanese students based on her personal experience, woke me up.

The theme of *proximity* is clearly present as we imagine our Lesley students embarking on global internships. Students can learn something about the culture of the place they will travel to, they can learn some things about themselves, but for much of their internship they will need to rely on flexibility and humility to establish connections and have a successful experience. *This* training can *only* happen in relationship—in an exchange and collaboration with others. The combination of *proximity/exchange with others and critical exploration of one's own background, assumptions and biases* will help all of our students establish a practice of cultural humility.

Exploring Bias

Nearly a year after having written a vignette describing my classroom experience with the Guyanese students, I had an opportunity to reflect on that piece of writing during a day-long retreat with our CLCI writers' group. The process was inspiring and also uncomfortable, as my unconscious and unexamined biases were illuminated. In the context of shared conversations, two significant shifts happened for me. First, I broadened my scope beyond the limits of the global internship setting, realizing that cultural humility could help *every* one of our students better prepare for *any* therapeutic encounter—whether in a "global" setting, or here in Cambridge. Second, I understood that before I could effectively help the students prepare for global experiences, I needed to be more fully engaged in the work of developing cultural humility myself, as I'd found statements in my vignette that were troubling in this regard. These statements are highlighted in the text below, from the original written vignette.

Vignette

Expertise

The classroom was filled with thirteen adult students in a self-designed masters' program, sitting at tables in groups of three or four. They had just spent 20 minutes or so out in the hallway, painting on the large brown paper sheets that were taped to the walls. *Yet as much as they'd enjoyed that process, it had not seemed to engage much depth of meaning for them.* Now they had returned to our room to begin their art-making anew, with a different material—the next in a series of various art materials my colleague was to offer them.

What happened as they began to engage this new material was both striking and illuminating. With barely an introduction or transition, each and every student immediately took up this new stuff and began to work with it. The men and the women in the group were equally skilled. They worked with ease, with confidence, and with a playful inventiveness. No longer the "expressive therapy experts," my colleague and I marveled as the silence in the room deepened, and the concentration, the sure familiarity of our students' own expertise, held sway. The students were on their own ground. This was an unexpected and magical moment. After the allotted time, we turned to a discussion of their process. *They spoke of memories, of their childhoods, of their homeland in Guyana.*

The art material that the students had been given on their return to the classroom was raffia: long strands of grass-like fiber derived from the stems of the large leaves of the raffia palm tree. It is a material that is more accessible at American craft stores than it is in Guyana. Although it was not exactly a material indigenous to their homeland, *the raffia was close enough to the grasses they had woven as schoolchildren.* Our students knew its properties, and were intimate with its processes. *They were invited into creativity, into making by the tactile, sensory material of their early experience.*

. . . The moment with the raffia stays with me. I was humbled by the quality of the environment that I experienced that day. The students' being at home in their endeavor created a completely different relationship to the classroom setting, to the work of engaging art materials, and to their instructors. In their creative process, everything had become integrated. *As they had connected to themselves, to each other, and to their home culture, an atmosphere of genuine healing pervaded the space.* The students had indeed created a home, and invited us into it.

Critical Inquiry

The italic passages in the vignette hold some implicit assumptions about meaning and healing that prompted my critical reflection. Clearly, I'd held certain aspects of the students' work in a kind of romanticized response that hovered around the edges of my consciousness, and limited my view. My experience in the room that day had been palpable, but the sharing in the classroom had been brief. In writing up the vignette, I stayed too comfortable in privileging my own interpretations rather than being more deeply curious about the students' *own* feelings and narratives. I needed to connect the dots, and bring in the voices of the students' personal experience.

Asking for Feedback

In June of 2014, shortly after the CLCI writing retreat, our group presented works in progress at the annual Institute. In offering my own piece, I included my process of critical inquiry, and the challenges of confronting my own assumptions. After I was finished, a colleague from another part of the university raised her hand. She suggested simply that I contact the students to see if any of them would give me their own feedback about the experience with the raffia. I was delighted and felt embarrassed that I hadn't thought of this, but I went right home and emailed the group who'd been back in Guyana since the previous summer. One member of the class responded.

Juanita's Experience

Juanita did experience the raffia as special and different from the other arts materials explored in the class, and she deeply investigated her own experience, recalled many months after the fact. She said (in part),

> When I saw the raffia grass which we call tibisri straw, I felt connected to it mostly because it is a very significant piece of material to my country since it is part of the traditional wear of the first/indigenous people of our dear land Guyana; the Amerindians. Seeing it in the USA in a classroom and being used for such a significant purpose was both surprising and fulfilling. I felt connected to this simple piece of material and immediately felt the urge to touch it.

Juanita describes her response to the material, and offers its Guyanese name. She locates it in the heritage of her home country, and describes her connection to it as mostly related to the historical and cultural significance of the material. It was gratifying for her to see this material in the context of our classroom. In my own focus on childhood associations, and lack of further inquiry, I had completely missed an opportunity to learn about Juanita's appreciation for the material's rich cultural association.

Juanita goes on:

> I remember the slightly rough but comforting feeling of the material as it glided around my fingers. For some strange reason it was captivating, I was in no hurry to stop. While playing with the material the thought of plaiting my daughters' hair surfaced but the irony in that is; I also feel helpless in that area. However and probably because this was play it felt different. *This thought of motherhood, the comforting feeling of the material and the exercising yet easy movement of the wrists created some amount of calmness.*

While my own assumptions had located the group members' experience of ease and calm in their re-connection to their own childhoods, Juanita is reminded of her adult mothering and caretaking of her own child, which she finds comforting and calming.

Finally, Juanita discusses her overall experience:

> I feel very helpless when participating in art exercises, despite my knowledge that it is more a therapeutic than a learning exercise. This feeling is not strange since it was the same feelings I had in High School when trying to complete my Biology assignments. Therefore when the change came and *I realized I can do something with this material . . . It was all about doing what I felt like doing in that moment, no one was judging what I did, there were no instructions to follow. I did what came to mind and it felt great!*

Juanita expresses a moment of change: when she feels pleasure in mastery, and feels freed from judgment or shame. She was able to *do* something with the material, without instruction. Perhaps this was one source of that "atmosphere of genuine healing" that I'd been blind to.

Juanita's feedback shifts the voice of my own projections (based largely on my own nonverbal experience) to the voice of one who actually encountered the material, and helped to create the true "healing atmosphere" by her own involvement. In a 2009 Ted Talk, novelist Chimamanda Ngozi Adichie (2009) describes the "danger of a single story," where narrow assumptions about the other limit one's view to a personally biased narrative. I believe I'd fallen under the sway of such assumptions, narrowly romanticizing the connection to childhood prompted by the use of a certain material. In emphasizing this aspect of their experience, I failed to appreciate the adults in the room. Some of my original statements now feel to me reminiscent of the paternalistic attitudes that my mother and many white women of her generation brought to their efforts to be of service. A white professor teaching a course with thirteen students of color, I had unconsciously limited my view of the students and the fullness of their expression.

Identity and Context

As a white Caucasian woman, I am representative of my profession; most of my fellows are also from the dominant culture. Both the American Art Therapy Association (AATA) and the American Music Therapy Association (AMTA) found that their membership self-reported at about 89 percent Caucasian, and between 90–94 percent female in surveys conducted in 2011. The student population in Lesley's Graduate School of Arts and Social Sciences (where the Expressive Therapies Division is housed) reflected about this same percentage for 2011–2012. The Caucasian dominance of our field and in Lesley's program needs to be firmly held in view as we attempt to prepare our students for their work—at home or in global internships.

In the expressive therapies, arts-based process is situated in a particular context: there are layers of meaning involved that may challenge the students' assumptions about various aspects of the work. While therapeutic work in the arts is often cited as helpful across many cultures by virtue of its "universality," it is worth remembering the specificity of our approach and point of view. Dan Hocoy (2002, p. 141), an art therapist, identifies a core question for us in this passage:

> Although art therapy is regarded by some (e.g., Kalish-Weiss, 1989) as being less culture bound than other therapeutic modalities as it is less encumbered by linguistic expression, art therapy remains culturally and historically situated. (This) fact . . . is easily missed because the culture from which it originates is also the dominant culture of the U.S. (e.g., Greenfield, 1997), and as such, it is as invisible as the air one breathes.

Any of the creative arts therapies (whether based in music, dance, drama, or the visual arts) will use a vocabulary of materials that shape the therapeutic encounter. The specific qualities of any given material might or might not support healing for a particular group or individual. When Juanita found a sense of calm and comfort in our classroom, the raffia had helped to engender those feelings, based on her personal experience. Offered an array of possibilities, both familiar and unfamiliar, our students will find a field in which to examine their judgments concerning "good" or "bad" materials. Can styrofoam promote healing? Who is to say? Such questions may throw open the gates of creativity, and may also ground students in the essential view that any and all materials and processes are situated in a context, and that preferences, including the therapist's, are shaped by the personal, historical, and cultural identity of each individual. Discussion of materials may then become a prelude to important conversations about how we sometimes "other" those we would like to "help." My own experience reflects this deepening process. Initially, I was focused on the responses of my students to a specific material, but in the context of peer conversations, my attention shifted to a more personal examination of racial bias. "Trust the process!" has been the motto in our expressive therapies program since it took shape in the 1970s. I might suggest an amendment: "trust the process—and investigate your underlying assumptions!"

Conclusion

A month after attending the Cultural Literacy Curriculum Institute of 2013, I found myself teaching an expressive therapies course with thirteen students from Guyana. Looking back at my description of the students as they engaged the arts process, I identified implicit assumptions that I'd made about the way the material was affecting them, which narrowed my thinking and prevented me from being more curious. When one student shared her fuller experience with me, she offered a rich and meaningful narrative: the "thick" world of her specific human life.

In recent years, the ongoing tragic injustices of racial bias are becoming more visible at the national level. The view of cultural humility is critically important, whether abroad or here at home. As a child of social activists, I had the advantage of an unusually supportive family culture, and still my own racism and cultural bias are lurking in my unexamined and habitual thinking. It is uncomfortable to confront these places—and yet this same discomfort gives me hope for transformation, for it arises from, and helps me to lift up, the part of me that appreciates and values simple justice.

We need to encourage ourselves and each other to participate in, support, promote, and create opportunities for *proximity/exchange with others and critical exploration of our own backgrounds, assumptions and biases.* I have found the peer support of a diverse group of university colleagues to be of inestimable value, and I also hope to share elements of this recent personal inquiry with my students. If my teaching is authentically grounded in my own ongoing self-examination, I have the possibility of better supporting students in their own developmental journeys.

Questions for Reflection

1. What part of your personal process might be useful to share with students in order to help them self-reflect regarding the values of cultural humility?
2. What specific topics, theories, materials, or processes in your discipline might provide an initial pathway for students to begin to examine culturally biased assumptions?
3. Where do you see the influence of proximity as having played a role in perpetuating or challenging bias in your own life? How has this influence shown up in your teaching?

References

Adichie, C. N. (2009, July). *The danger of a single story* [video file]. Retrieved from https://www.ted.com/talks/chimamanda_adichie_the_danger_of_a_single_story

Hocoy, D. (2002). Cross-cultural issues in art therapy. *Art Therapy, 19*(4), 141–145. doi:10.1080/07421656.2002.10129683

Satir, V. (2000). The therapist story. In Baldwin, M. ed. *The use of self in therapy* (2nd ed.). New York, NY. Haworth Press.

11 Looking In and Acting Out

A Personal Search for Inclusive Pedagogical Practice

Janet Sauer

Looking In

It is difficult for me to determine when exactly my interest in inclusive pedagogy began. It may have been when I discovered one of my high school students could not read aloud from the script the class was performing. I was teaching video production in what was then a unique bilingual/bicultural community-run school in the Navajo Reservation in the early '90s. Nearly half of my students were dominant Navajo language speakers as were most of my colleagues, many of whom came from the local community. The school's successful bilingual program was based on Cummin's "context-embedded" experiences for English as a Second Language (ESL) instruction (Reyher, 1990), and all of my students were reading and writing in both Navajo and English, except this youth. I could not recall ever having met someone who did not read and I suddenly realized this student was not a typical English language learner (ELL). I was not an ELL teacher, nor was I a special education teacher yet, and I did not know the first thing about teaching students "like him." It was my first real teaching job, and I wanted all of my students to find purpose and value in their education. I had recently returned from living three years in Botswana, Africa, as a Peace Corps Volunteer. There I began to learn about prejudice and privilege in a more global context. My experiences working for the Ministry of Education and witnessing the repercussions of cultural and physical genocide on the African continent started to inform my thinking and teaching in the United States. I learned about the ethnocentric and hegemonic structures manifested in our educational system particularly regarding indigenous peoples. Now, more than twenty-five years later, I am in the position of preparing future teachers to work with students who are in many ways like the youth on the Reservation who I had "othered." I approach teacher education from an interdisciplinary perspective in which we examine ways to support the learning of all children and youth, particularly those othered by the social, political, and cultural institutions of the American educational system.

In Botswana, Africa, in the late 1980s I witnessed local teachers and missionaries creatively work with small impoverished rural communities of the Kalahari Desert to educate their children, with and without physical impairments. I grappled with my Whiteness and privilege. Occasionally while walking in a village, I heard "Makgoa," a pejorative for White people that changed the prefix from Lekgoa for a Caucasian person to a thing; some Batswana friends told me it roughly translates to mean throw-up from the sea. I am a fair-skinned, light-haired Midwesterner with Irish/English ancestry. Many Botswana children walked barefoot for miles to attend school, and I was repeatedly asked to take a child back home with me to the United States in hopes of a better life. During my service time I traveled to apartheid South Africa. The African National Congress called that year (1988) "The Year of United Action for People's Power." Nelson Mandela was still imprisoned, and songs calling for his freedom could be heard on the radio. I was shocked to see the level of racial injustice experienced by the indigenous Black people of South Africa, living so close to me and the democracy of Botswana. It is equally troubling now to find that more than twenty years after South Africa ended apartheid in 1994, and sixty years after *Brown v. Board of Education* was thought to have ended segregated schools in the U.S., racial equity and justice continue to challenge structures and relationships within our country. As a child of the civil rights era raised with a commitment for social justice, it is timely (if not long overdue) that I join my colleagues in examining our own inclusive pedagogy.

What is meant by *inclusive pedagogy*? Pedagogy is defined by the Merriam-Webster Dictionary as "the art, science, or profession of teaching." Teaching and learning are intertwined social acts, and as a teacher of preservice educational and therapeutic professionals, my pedagogy needs to reflect inclusive values through modeling and creating a safe space in which my students can examine their own assumptions and attitudes. An important part of my work is to support my students in building their own understanding of inclusion. *Inclusion* for me is a value-ridden word and a lived experience as an inclusion advocate for the children I taught as an elementary special education teacher, and later as a mother of a child born with Down syndrome. Inclusion is not limited to constructs of race and ethnicity, gender, age, or dis/ability labels. Inclusion indicates valued membership in a social group regardless of identity markers.

Inclusion means valuing human diversity. Diversity is thought of not only in its biological sense, but also in a social sense, and some have argued that it has philosophical roots going as far back as the pre-Socratics (Lafaye & Cabrero, 2010). Over time, Lafaye and Cabrero (2010) explain, philosophers have sought an ethical foundation "that would provide justice, equality, and freedom to society" (p. 97) based on a universal reason and respect for diversity, but these efforts have been largely lost to the tendency for groups to continually differentiate themselves and, inevitably, "a part of human diversity has usually been left out" (p. 98), namely those we think of in terms of *disabled*. I approach the topic of inclusion from an intersectional lens that recognizes the interconnected, interdependent, and/or overlapping nature of social categorizations (Crenshaw, 1991). I know my child's maleness, Whiteness, and middle-class suburban identities intersect with his dis/ability, just as identity markers influence me and my students' experiences.

Acting Out

One of the reasons I work at Lesley University (LU) is its commitment to social justice. I participated in the Cultural Literacy Curriculum Institute (CLCI) the first chance I had. The focus was on indigenous cultures, and I was introduced to the concept of cultural humility, the "ability to maintain an interpersonal stance that is other-oriented (or open to the other) in relation to aspects of cultural identity that are most important to the [person]" (Hook, Davis, Owen, Worthington, & Utsey, 2013, p. 2). I quickly felt I belonged to this group of colleagues who sought to examine our own sociocultural experiences and to embrace cultural humility in our professional practices. The LU Core Value of Diversity states, "Through their varied learning experiences, Lesley students develop the tools to effectively interact with diverse populations and strive for social justice and equity" (NEASC Self-Study, 2014, p. 4). But I know tackling issues of racism and ableism for social justice and equity is complicated. In a diversity training workshop I did with the LU student leaders group on campus (September 20, 2014), I pointed out that the Office of Equal Opportunity and Inclusion (OEOI) guides Lesley in achieving our educational mission and nurturing the university's four core values (inquiry, community, diversity, and citizenship). I emphasized how these values are interrelated and thus go beyond race and religion to include other identities like dis/ability. I taught these students about ableism:

> [the] devaluation of disability [that] results in societal attitudes that uncritically assert that it is better for a child to walk than roll, speak than sign, read print than Braille, spell independently than use a spell-check, and hang out with nondisabled kids as opposed to other disabled kids.
>
> (Hehir, 2003, p. 1)

I was pleased that these students were quick to acknowledge the similar inequities experienced between people with disabilities and those from more commonly discussed marginalized minority groups.

Educational researchers of K–12 inclusive education Jorgensen and colleagues (Jorgensen & Lambert, 2012; Jorgensen, McSheehan, &

Sonnenmeier, 2010) designed "Beyond Access," a professional development curriculum model in which they explain "inclusion means more than just being *in*" (Jorgensen & Lambert, 2012). In their list of key components for planning and implementing inclusive education for students with disabilities, they describe the importance of the *attitude* of the adult support team members as "presuming competence" of the children because "it is far more dangerous to presume that students will never learn and then find out that they might have, had they been provided with high quality instruction and assistive technology to support their communication and literacy skills" (Jorgensen & Lambert, 2012, p. 28). Jorgensen is part of an ever-increasing cohort of scholars who have shown through research what many family advocates have argued for decades: that even children with the most significant disabilities *and* their typical peers *can* and *do* learn alongside each other (Kliewer, Biklen, & Petersen, 2015). We have come to recognize how individualized education plans that are developed focusing only on the *placement* or *location* of the child, something that is typically reflected in percentage of time spent in a general education classroom, is shortsighted. Inclusion is far more than "being in." Inclusion means valuing the individuality of each community member, with all of his/her/their various identities. In her article about inclusive pedagogy, Harwood (2010) explains "difference is itself at the very heart of what constitutes our humanity" (p. 358). It is this idea that my inclusive pedagogy tries to teach: that people with disabilities are not something *other* than *us*; they *are* us.

When I teach about the positive implications of inclusion for children and youth with disabilities, I try to model inclusive pedagogy in my own practice. I include the voices of people with disabilities in my classes through guest visits, videos, and autobiographies. Many of these stories illustrate complex intersections between impairments that may or may not be disabling, and other identity markers. An increasing number of my own students "out themselves" as people labeled with disabilities that might not be otherwise visible. Rather than interviewing a stranger who experiences disability as part of the coursework, some of these students write self-portrait narratives about their experiences with prejudice and social stigmas that created barriers to their full membership in educational contexts and society in general. Many students remark in their evaluations how the course "opened my eyes" and "changed my perspective." Student reflections based on guests or field-based observations suggest many students' preconceived (limited) notions about disability were questioned. One student titled a paper, "Normalcy is overrated" (K.C., October 22, 2013), a common sentiment that emerges in class discussions.

Some of my students, however, challenge inclusion as being "unrealistic." One of my students wrote in her Personal Statement, "Special-ed. liberalism has not accomplished as much as we think" (R. S., June 5, 2015). She described how despite her privileged upbringing, she felt isolated as a youth with a neurologic disability. While I encourage discussions of inclusion with regard to race, ethnicity, religion, and socioeconomic status, my mention of gender was limited to the male/female binary. Then after class one day a few students lingered to ask me why the self-advocate author Jonathan Mooney (2007) used the pronoun "he" to describe a person in his book who was transgender, arguing that it was counterproductive to his research question: What is normal? We followed up the conversation with a whole-class discussion about gender fluidity—the discourse and systematic discrimination against transgender people. These students brought to light my own limited understanding of diversity, and I went looking to my colleagues and the students to learn and reflect once again about how I might improve my inclusive practice.

Inclusive Pedagogy in Practice

My education students go into the community for their practicum and experience segregated schools every day. They frequently ask why what they see in the field does not reflect professional expectations regarding culturally responsive teachers (Villegas & Lucas, 2002) and inclusive education. Since I teach about the intersectionality between culture, race, and concepts of dis/ability, in my classes we discuss the 30th Annual Report to Congress on the Implementation of the Individuals with Disabilities Education Act, 2008 (U.S. Department of Education, Office of Special Education and Rehabilitation Services, 2011) that explains how we have "disproportionate representation of racial and ethnic groups in specific disability categories that was the result of inappropriate identification" (p. 157). I also share the Review of Special Education in the Commonwealth of Massachusetts (Hehir, Grindal, & Eidelman, 2012) that outlines local trends:

> Massachusetts has the second highest rate of special education identification in the United States . . . Low-income students with disabilities and Latino and African American students with disabilities are considerably less likely to be included in general education classes when compared to their White and Asian special education counterparts . . . We find evidence that among special education students, lack of integration may be a contributing factor for lower performance on the MCAS (Massachusetts Comprehensive Assessment System).
>
> (p. 1)

While I only recently moved to the Boston area, it hasn't taken me long to hear the stories of parents of children of color illustrating some of the systemic segregated practices in schools.

The guests I have join my classes share their stories and help my students understand the connections between race, culture, language, and special education for young people with disabilities and their families. For instance, I arranged to have Saba (all names are pseudonyms), a Chinese American, come to class and discuss with us her experiences as the mother of two-year-old An, who received early intervention for speech and language. In another class, Margie, an eighteen-year-old African American with intellectual disabilities, described her experience taking classes at UMass Boston. She was joined by the Special Education administrator and transition coordinator from a Boston public high school, as well as a professor who works on the Think College project, a national initiative to promote access to higher education for people with intellectual disabilities. Other guests included Maria, a Latina mother of twelve-year-old Eduardo, who is labeled with autism; Maho, a recent immigrant from Vietnam and the mother of an eleven-year-old daughter diagnosed with a chromosomal duplication; David, an African American male who was born in the South and did not talk until he was four; Lisa, an African American mother whose teenaged daughter Sarah has been labeled with autism, Down syndrome, and a mood disorder; and Anita, a first-generation American whose family emigrated from India. Her third son, Sameer, is sixteen years old and labeled with Asperger's syndrome. After modeling the informal interviews in my classes, the students are assigned to go out into the community and talk with a person with a disability and/or their family member(s). In response, my students often comment about the powerful impact these informal conversations have had on their understandings of our course readings. One student noted that the interview was "insightful in more ways than I could have anticipated." The influence of these conversations is hard to measure, but I take notice when the students change the classroom discourse and refer to people with disabilities they meet simply as "a person" rather than describing them based on their disability labels.

Culturally and linguistically diverse (CLD) families do not typically experience collaborative partnerships with their children's school professionals. Despite its successes in achieving compulsory public education for students with disabilities, the Individuals with Disabilities Education Act (IDEA) is implemented by a bureaucratic system that demands parents to become advocates for their individual children through negotiations reliant upon on social and cultural capital, but CLD families may not advocate in this way (Bacon & Causton-Theoharis, 2013; Harry, 2008; Olivos, Gallagher, & Aguilar, 2010; Sauer & Albanesi, 2013). CLD families face many barriers from schools to such participation and advocacy, ranging from prejudice and unprofessionalism to lack of cultural awareness and inappropriate or unavailable accommodations related to language. In studies of participation at individualized education program (IEP) meetings, CLD families attended most meetings but were not provided opportunities to contribute; the lack of opportunity was most frequently attributed to hierarchical power relations and marginalization of families (Klingner & Harry, 2006; Lo, 2008; Salas, 2004; Wagner, Newman, Cameto, Javitz, & Valdes, 2012). Parents' rights documents and IEPs have been evaluated and found to be written in ways that are difficult to understand, especially for CLD families (Fitzgerald & Watkins, 2006; Lo, 2014; Rossetti, Sauer, & Bui, in press). Materials are not routinely translated or translated in time for meetings, and skilled interpreters are not consistently provided at "team" meetings despite being federally mandated (Klingner & Harry, 2006; Lo, 2008).

Without family participation and collaborative partnerships between families and schools, CLD students are vulnerable to lesser quality and more segregated education programs, as well as faulty diagnostic processes resulting in disproportionate representation in special education (Burke, 2013; Harry & Klingner, 2006). The percentage of students with disabilities engaged in inclusive education at urban public schools has been as low as 10 percent of the special education population, and problems of disproportionate representation in special education and performance gaps among African American, Hispanic, and White students persist (Artiles & Kozleski, 2007). In Massachusetts, low-income students with disabilities and African American and Latino students with disabilities were found to be considerably less likely to be included in general education classes compared to White and Asian students with disabilities (Hehir et al., 2012).

Conclusion

It is clear that we have a lot of work to do as we move toward inclusive and equitable education. The President of the Global Perspective Institute and senior fellow at the Association of American Colleges and Universities, Larry Breskamp (2011), argues that now is the time for action in Institutes of Higher Education (IHE)—that faculty "need to reexamine our roles in preparing citizens for participation in both our democratic society and the larger community" (p. 2) to respond to an increasingly diverse society by working in collaboration with our communities. This chapter described some of my efforts to infuse social justice into my practice, and support my students' development of cultural humility and an understanding that inclusive education is more than empathy for children and youth with disabilities, but a civil right because "injustice anywhere is a threat to justice everywhere" (Martin Luther King, Jr., 1963). Critical thinking and the concepts of ableism (social construction of disability) and privilege challenge those of us in higher education who try to model inclusive pedagogy for our students who might be more familiar with traditional didactic instruction. We need to critically reflect upon the events and situations of our own personal experiences and those of our students by looking within ourselves in order to move forward and act out on behalf of social justice. Although I witnessed some of the most terrible segregation in apartheid, South Africa, I did not see my ablest attitude toward the Native American youth I taught on the Navajo Reservation, nor did I anticipate the discussion about normalcy to include transgender discrimination in my class about children with disabilities.

The timing seems right (if not overdue) for IHEs to reposition ourselves as social justice leaders who can manage the praxis between theory and practice of inclusive pedagogy alongside our students. The Black Lives Matter movement and the recent first Disability Pride Parade are illustrative of current social justice actions, the context in which our students are becoming adult democratic citizens. While my efforts in my own classes are quite modest in the face of current events, I hope my description of some of my work might inform others with similar inclinations about ways we can contribute to positive change.

Questions for Reflection

1. Which social/physical identities are most salient in your life? How do these influence the way you develop and plan your courses?
2. Describe your experience in inclusive teaching with special needs college students. What have been positive aspects of that experience? What have been the challenges?
3. In what ways do you see the intersection of dis/ability, race, ethnicity, religion, and gender playing out in your institution?

References

Artiles, A. J., & Kozleski, E. B. (2007). Beyond convictions: Interrogating culture, history, and power in inclusive education. *Language Arts, 84,* 357–364.

Bacon, J. K., & Causton-Theoharis, J. (2013). "It should be teamwork": A critical investigation of school practices and parent advocacy in special education. *International Journal of Inclusive Education, 17,* 682–699. doi:10.1080/13603116.2012.708060

Breskamp, L. A. (2011). Higher education for civic learning and democratic engagement: Reinvesting in longstanding commitments. *Diversity & Democracy, 14*(3), 1–3.

Burke, M. M. (2013). Improving parental involvement: Training special education advocates. *Journal of Disability Policy Studies, 23,* 225–234. doi:10.1177/1044207311424910

Crenshaw, K. (1991). Mapping the margins: Intersectionality, identity politics, and violence against women of color. *Stanford Law Review, 43*(6), 1241–1299. Retrieved from http://www.jstor.org/stable/1229039

Fitzgerald, J., & Watkins, M. W. (2006). Parents' rights in special education: The readability of procedural safeguards. *Exceptional Children, 72,* 497–510.

Harry, B. (2008). Collaboration with culturally and linguistically diverse families: Ideal versus reality. *Exceptional Children, 74*, 372–388.

Harry, B., & Klingner, J. (2006). *Why are so many minority students in special education? Understanding race and disability in schools.* New York, NY: Teachers College Press.

Harwood, V. (2010). The place of imagination in inclusive pedagogy: Thinking with Maxine Greene and Hannah Arendt. *International Journal of Inclusive Education, 14*(4), 357–369. doi:10.1080/13603110802504572

Hehir, T. (2003). Beyond inclusion: Educator's "ableist" assumptions about students with disabilities compromise the quality of instruction. *School Administrator, 60*(3), 36–40.

Hehir, T., Grindal, T., & Eidelman, H. (2012). *Review of special education in the Commonwealth of Massachusetts.* Retrieved from http://www.doe.mass.edu/sped/hehir/2014-09synthesis.pdf

Hook, J. N., Davis, D. E., Owen, J., Worthington, E. L., Jr., & Utsey, S. O. (2013). Cultural humility: Measuring openness to culturally diverse clients. *Journal of Counseling Psychology, 60*, 353–366. doi:10.1037/a0032595

Jorgensen, C. M., & Lambert, L. (2012). Inclusion means more than just being "in": Planning full participation of students with intellectual and other developmental disabilities in the general education classroom. *International Journal of Whole Schooling, 8*(2), 21–35.

Jorgensen, C. M., McSheehan, M., & Sonnenmeier, R. M. (2010). *The beyond access model: Promoting membership, participation, and learning for students with disabilities in the general education classroom.* Baltimore: Paul A. Brookes Publishing Co.

King, M. L. (1963, April 16). Letter from a Birmingham City Jail. Retrieved from http://teachingamericanhistory.org/library/document/letter-from-birmingham-city-jail/

Kliewer, C., Biklen, D., & Petersen, A. (2015). *The end of intellectual disability.* New York, NY: Teachers College Press.

Klingner, J. K., & Harry, B. (2006). The special education referral and decision-making process for English language learners: Child study team meetings and placement conferences. *Teachers College Record, 108*, 2247–2281.

Lafaye, C. G. and Cabrero, J. R. (2010). Diversity ethics. An alternative to Peter Singer's ethics. *Dilemata, 2*(2), 95–116.

Lesley University (2015). Lesley University self-study report. Prepared for the accreditation visit of the Commission on Institutions of Higher Education of the New England Association of Schools and Colleges, (NEASC). Cambridge, MA. April 12-15, 2015.

Lo, L. (2008). Chinese families' level of participation and experiences in IEP meetings. *Preventing School Failure, 53*, 21–27. doi:10.3200/PSFL.53.1.21–27

Lo, L. (2014). Readability of individualized education programs. *Preventing School Failure, 58*, 96–102. doi:10.1080/1045988X.2013.782532

Mooney, J. (2007). *The short bus: A journey beyond normal.* New York: Henry Holt and Company, LLC.

Olivos, E. M., Gallagher, R. J., & Aguilar, J. (2010). Fostering collaboration with culturally and linguistically diverse families of children with moderate to severe disabilities. *Journal of Educational and Psychological Consultation, 20*, 28–40. doi:10.1080/10474410903535372

Reyhner, J. (1990). Effective language education practices and native language survival. In J. Reyhner (Ed.), *A description of the rock point community school bilingual education program* (pp. 95–106). Choctaw, OK: Native American Language Issues.

Rossetti, Z., Sauer, J., & Bui, O. (in press). Developing collaborative partnerships with culturally and linguistically diverse families during the IEP process. *Teaching Exceptional Children.*

Salas, L. (2004). Individualized Educational Plan (IEP) meetings and Mexican American parents: Let's talk about it. *Journal of Latinos and Education, 3*, 181–192. doi:10.1207/s1532771xjle0303_4

Sauer, J., & Albanesi, H. (2013). Questioning privilege from within the special education process. *Understanding & Dismantling Privilege, 3*(1), 1–21.

Stoner, J. B., Bock, S. J., Thompson, J. R., Angell, M. E., Heyl, B. S., & Crowley, E. P. (2005). Welcome to our world: Parent perceptions of interactions between parents of young children with ASD and education professionals. *Focus on Autism and Other Developmental Disabilities, 20*, 39–51.

U.S. Department of Education, Office of Special Education and Rehabilitation Services. (2011). *30th Annual Report to Congress on the Implementation of the Individuals with Disabilities Education Act.* Washington, D.C. Report Contract No. ED06 CO0062.

Villegas, A. M. & Lucas, T. (2002). Preparing culturally responsive teachers: Rethinking the curriculum. *Journal of Teacher Education, 53*(1), 20–32.

Wagner, M., Newman, L., Cameto, R., Javitz, H., & Valdes, K. (2012). A national picture of parent and youth participation in IEP and transition planning meetings. *Journal of Disability Policy Studies, 23*, 140–155. doi:10.1177/1044207311425384

Reflection Activities

Reflection I. Where I'm From

(Adapted from the poem "Where I'm From" by George Ella Lyon)

Read the poems in Chapter 9. Notice the kinds of images that make up the poems.

Spend ten minutes creating a list of people, smells, sights, memories, and foods from your childhood/youth.

Take another ten to fifteen minutes editing and arranging and adding to this list, in an "I'm from . . ." pattern.

If a group is doing this activity, those who wish may read their poems aloud.

Answer the following questions to continue your reflection, either in small groups of three or four or individually, through further journaling:

1. Where are you from, in terms of race, ethnicity, gender, socio-economic status, religion, sexual orientation, and physical/mental able-ness?
2. What are some of the strengths and challenges about growing up with these social identities?
3. What aspects of this social identity are most important to you right now?

Journal Space:

Reflection II. Steppingstones in Responding to Difference

Take a few minutes to write down five or six individuals or events that have led to your understanding of and experience with diversity/difference. Observe the flow of choices and events, directions, and detours that your personal and vocational life has taken.

Feel free to take some paper and markers and draw out these steps as stones or a map that represents your journey.

Notice if there are any threads running through your steps.

Discuss your experiences and insights in small and/or large group.

Journal Space:

Reflection III. Exploring Power in Leadership

Now power properly understood is nothing but the ability to achieve purpose. . .

. . . And one of the great problems of history is that the concepts of love and power have usually been contrasted as opposites—polar opposites—so that love is identified with a resignation of power, and power with a denial of love.

. . . We've got to get this thing right. What is needed is a realization that power without love is reckless and abusive, and love without power is sentimental and anemic. Power at its best is love implementing the demands of justice, and justice at its best is power correcting everything that stands against love . . .

. . . It is precisely this collision of immoral power with powerless morality that constitutes the major crisis of our times.

Rev. Martin Luther King, Jr. Presidential address at the Southern
Christian Leadership Conference, August 16, 1967

Read Martin Luther King, Jr.'s statement, and journal on the following questions (or what stands out for you in his words):

Describe a time when you exercised power in a teaching situation. In what ways does the situation fit King's definitions? How was power and love expressed?

Mentors and advisors often wield strong power. In your life, what kind of power have you experienced from a mentor or advisor? What kind of power/love have you shown?

Journal Space:

Notes for Engaging Discussions

Culturally Responsive Teaching and Cultural Humility

As many readers know, when colleagues gather to discuss a topic, especially one that is sensitive or for which people care deeply, a recognized and agreed-upon structure can aid in keeping the time safe and effective. While there are many ways to achieve these goals, we recommend a process with three steps:

1. Guidelines

Begin with guidelines the group agrees to follow. Our guidelines were developed at the Center for Courage and Renewal, and we found them important to our learning and open discussion. These form a strong container for conversation. Your group may have its own guidelines, or draw from these:

- Come to the work with all of the self
- Presume welcome and extend welcome
- Participation is an invitation, an opportunity, not a demand
- NO FIXING, advising, or setting straight
- When the going gets rough, turn to wonder
- Listen to the silence
- Turn to nature for insight and inspiration
- Let our time together remain confidential within the group
- Consider that it's possible to emerge from our time together refreshed

2. Conversation Structure

Establish the time with a clear opening and closing.

> Openings: Sit in a circle if possible, or at tables where everyone can see each other. Start with a minute of silence, or read a poem, or check in

by asking each person to say a word that describes how they are feeling or what they hope for the group.

Closing: Allow enough time to bring the discussion to a clear ending. People might offer a statement about how they are feeling or words of gratitude, read a poem, or sit for a closing moment of silence.

3. Alternatives to Large Group Discussion

When using reflective questions, it can be powerful for each person to journal, draw, or sit quietly with the question before the larger discussion starts. People can also meet in small groups of two, three, or four to discuss, where each person has a time to speak before the larger group convenes.

Art, music, and movement are wonderful ways to explore questions, learning, and feelings in metaphorical, nonlinear ways!

Contributor Biographies

Meenakshi Chhabra is Associate Professor in the Global Interdisciplinary Studies Program. She is a Fulbright Senior Scholar and also recognized as a Fulbright Specialist in Peace and Conflict. As a scholar and a practitioner, Dr. Chhabra has conducted extensive research and practice related to peace education in conflict and post-conflict contexts, both nationally and internationally.

Sharlene Voogd Cochrane's interest in social and cultural history, especially intersections of race, gender, and religion, led to research and writing on the racial integration of the YWCA and aspects of her family history. Former Dean of Faculty, she has published "Courage in the Academy: Sustaining the Heart of College and University Faculty." (2013). *Journal of Faculty Development, 27*(1), 28–34. Cochrane served as part of the Design Team and Faculty Leadership for the CLCI.

M. Francine Jennings teaches Integrated Teaching through the Arts, with a focus on Creative Movement, Critical Action Research, Diversity, and Reflective Thinking. She also performs her own one-woman show, highlighting the life of Harriet Tubman. Recent publications include: "Confronting Social Justice Issues Through the Lens of Arts Integration." In L. Drakeford (Ed.), *The Race Controversy in American Education.* Manuscript submitted.

Marjorie A. Jones's specialties include Teaching in Diverse Settings, Culturally Responsive Teaching, Cultural Studies, and Writing. Her publications include: (2011). "Building Agency Through Writing." In A. Dallalfar, E. Kingston-Mann, & T. Sieber (Eds.), *Transforming Classroom Culture: Inclusive Pedagogical Strategies.* New York: Palgrave Macmillan. Jones served as part of the Design Team and Faculty Leadership for the CLCI.

Michaela Kirby is an art therapist, psychologist, and educator and teaches courses in the Expressive Therapies Program. She is co-founder of a fiber arts studio exploring issues around women's sexuality. Kirby maintains a private practice and was recently elected to the Board of Directors of the American Art Therapy Association.

Coleen O'Connell is Director of the Ecological Teaching and Learning MS Program, teaches Graduate Education courses, and serves within the STEM Science division. She has had a lifelong relationship with various Native American cultures. In addition to many speaking engagements, O'Connell was the Maine Environmental Educator of the Year in 2013.

Janet Sauer teaches Education courses, focusing on Special Education, Disability Studies, and Family Engagement. Publications include: (2013). "Multiple Identities, Shifting Landscapes." In D. Lawrence-Brown & M. Sapon-Shevin (Eds.), *Condition Critical: Key Principles for Equitable and Inclusive Education.* New York: Teachers College Press.

Deborah Spragg, a musician as well as a licensed mental health counselor, and is Assistant Professor and Director of Field Training in the Expressive Therapies Division at Lesley University. She is a contributor to (2001). "Peer Supervision in the Development of the New Music and Expressive Therapist." In M. Forinash (Ed.), *Music Therapy Supervision.* Gilsum, NH: Barcelona.

Julie A. Stanwood serves as Assistant Dean of Academic Affairs for the College of Art and Design, and teaches undergraduate Psychology courses. She has published (2012). *An Investigation of Retention Factors for Visual Art Students.* Fort Lauderdale, FL: Nova Southeastern University.

Deborah D. Wright currently serves as Dean of the College of Professional and Continuing Education at Wentworth Institute of Technology. She was formerly Director of the Lesley Center for the Adult Learner. Her academic focus includes adult learning and courses like "Lives in Context," and she also teaches leadership, business management, and communication.

Index